Twayne's English Authors Series

Sylvia E. Bowman, *Editor*

INDIANA UNIVERSITY

C. Day Lewis

TEAS 124

C. DAY LEWIS

by JOSEPH N. RIDDEL
State University of New York at Buffalo

Twayne Publishers, Inc. : : New York

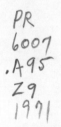

For the Memory of
Hunter Whiting

ACKNOWLEDGMENTS

For permission to quote copyrighted material, I am obligated to the following: C. Day Lewis, Jonathan Cape, Ltd., the Hogarth Press, for quotations from *Collected Poems 1954*; Jonathan Cape for Day Lewis' *The Poetic Image, Pegasus and Other Poems. The Gate and Other Poems* and *The Rock and Other Poems;* Basil Blackwell, Publisher, for *A Hope for Poetry;* the Harvard University Press for *The Lyric Impulse;* Harold Matson Company, Inc., agent for the author, for distribution rights in the United States and its possessions, and Philippine Islands.

I would like to thank the Research Foundation of Duke University for a Summer Research Fellowship in 1963, during which I first explored the subject of the Auden Group and the theoretical problems of poetry in the 1930's; and the Research Foundation of the State University of New York for fellowships during the summers of 1966 and 1967, when the book was written.

PREFACE

WHEN Cecil Day Lewis became Poet Laureate of Great Britain in 1968, he had been a considerable figure in British letters for nearly four decades; yet there has been no book of criticism assessing his achievement. There is, of course, a substantial body of criticism of Day Lewis' work, but it almost invariably considers him in relation to the far more significant achievement of W. H. Auden—and thus as a member of the so-called Auden Group—or as a political or radical poet whose major phase was restricted largely to a brief period in the 1930's when both the history of his culture and the tradition of its poetry seemed near to an apocalyptic end. Day Lewis, in other words, has seldom been regarded as an original poet in his own right; rather, his accomplishments have been considered as part of what was once thought to be a major revolution in English poetry and what now seems to be merely a historical convulsion which left only slight, though indelible, imprints on the tradition. But like Auden, who is demonstrably the more original poet, Day Lewis cannot be considered merely the phenomenon of one very limited historical period. If for a very brief time indeed (between, say, 1929 and 1935) he seemed to be one of the two or three preeminent young poets in England, offering a new style for a rapidly arriving new age, he now appears to be a minor poet, in the sense of a derivative and conservatively traditional poet, whose best work is continuous with its ancestry. In that time of historical crisis, Day Lewis and the "Auden Group" could think of themselves as heralds of a dawning new age, of a vague, somewhat ominous future like that projected in Yeats' "The Second Coming," an age discontinuous with the past except that it had extracted from the past those enduring monuments which transcend history and turned them dialectically in a new direction. But this illusion of radical discontinuity as the only possible way out of the historical vortex lasted for only a brief time. Day Lewis, perhaps more than any other so-called radical poet of his time, was not radical—in either style or theme. And his latter-day nomination to the Poet Laureateship is perhaps testimony enough to the accommodations he finally made with his cultural heritage.

This book is primarily an introduction to Day Lewis' poetry and the thought which lies both behind and within it. As such, it deliberately omits a good deal that would go into any full assessment of this man of letters—not only does it play down biography, except as biography explicitly illuminates the inner edge of Day Lewis' poetic world, but it omits consideration of Day Lewis as a translator of the classics; as a writer of children's books; as the author, under the pseudonym of Nicholas Blake, of a number of detective stories; and perhaps most significant, as the author of three revealing though uneven novels, all composed in the late years of the 1930's while he himself was undergoing a political and spiritual conversion which led him quickly into the Communist party and out again. This study, then, for reasons both of strategy and space, is limited mainly to Day Lewis as poet, and to an examination of his theoretical and ideological changes as manifest in three more or less distinct phases of his career.

Because the study is primarily an introduction, I approach the poetry chronologically, with a major emphasis on the poems written in the 1930's and the implications of the critical writings in which Day Lewis rationalized his "radicalism." But the general argument of the book is that Day Lewis' apparent changes from political to personal (or from dialectical to lyrical) poet are more superficial than substantive and that, despite the apparent differences from his early to his late poems, his innate preoccupations remained virtually the same. The style of his response to these preoccupations (whether personal or ideological) can be seen, then, as an index of the pressures of contemporary history on the poet who discovers himself the heir to a tradition he can neither destroy nor revitalize, escape nor accommodate. A chronological study of Day Lewis' poetry risks the repetitiousness which lies at the heart of his work; for while his poetry apparently changed with the rapid changes of history, the intrinsic themes remained to be explored from a new perspective or with an altered (temporal) consciousness.

The emphasis of this study, then, is on the period from 1929 to 1938, during which Day Lewis wrote the substantial body of poetry which earned him the reputation as a major force in the transition of English poetry. The first chapter sets the theoretical implications of this "radical" or "transitional" poetry in the context of the ideological pressures with which Day Lewis contended from the time he matriculated at Oxford until the advent of World War II and it suggests how those pressures can be linked both to his experience as an adolescent in

Georgian (pre-World War I) England and to his mature years. The purpose is to show that Day Lewis' preoccupation with the "divided self" was the common denominator of "radical" poetry in the 1930's and not merely his own subjective or personal crisis, and that his discovery that his personal self-dislocation was an analogue for the political, social, and moral dilemmas of his immediate culture made possible a poetry that transcended private concerns. Chapters 2 through 4 treat the poems published between 1929 and 1938, the "radical" poetry as it were. Chapter 5 treats his poetry of the 1940's in terms of its movement away from political toward personal experience, as an index of the way alterations in ideological commitment tended to conceal the continuity between the public and the personal: his continuing search for "the buried day." Chapter 6 deals with his rather sparse work in the last two decades, or specifically after his last long poem, *An Italian Visit,* which was published in 1952; this later poetry is read in the context of Day Lewis' theoretical concerns with "the lyric impulse" as the enduring and timeless center of all poetry, the "impulse" which lifts poetry out of history. The concluding chapter is a redivivus in terms of the three significant books of criticism Day Lewis wrote during the three apparently distinct periods of his career. Once again, the concern is with the thematic continuity rather than the stylistic discontinuity of Day Lewis' poetry—and thus, to put the study in a larger perspective, to suggest that the relation of the poet to history, and the self to the other, is at best a problematic which poetry presents and questions but never resolves. For the real subject of this book is, as I believe is true of the real subject of Day Lewis' poems, the problematic of language itself, a perennial theme of poetry which becomes more critical when history, that mythical or fictional order of events, manifests itself as chaos. For history and language are coterminous, and a crisis in the structure of one means a crisis in the structure of the other—a radical discontinuity ensues. My indirect argument, to put it simply, is that there is no such thing as a political poetry, or a poetry simply focused on an ideological truth; but that, on the contrary, poetry is a questioning of language by means of language and thus must treat all points of view as a problematic. When language is brought into question, or brings itself into question, all ideas of order are challenged and new ones are demanded; thus, all ideas of the self, which are indeed fictions or imaginary creations and hence structures of language, are brought into question and must be reconstructed once more in relation to the "other." Day Lewis' poetry fulfills the circle of this quest for order, for a whole self and thus for a new language.

I have kept the metaphysical argument largely indirect, however, since the first obligation of this series is to present the author and his particular works. But the particular works are of a piece; they compose a pattern (a journey or quest) that may reveal to us the essential dilemma of the modern poet. For Day Lewis is a modern poet, I would argue, because he is so perplexed by his modernism, so preoccupied with the rediscovery of the origins which would spare him from the burden of having to be original. In this regard, the arc of his career is a circle, which I treat as a hermeneutical circle leading from its beginning toward an end that repeats its beginning. Along that arc are the individual poems, especially the long ones, which are hardly familiar to students, let alone specialists in modern poetry. It is my hope that, even if the argument of this study is missed or resisted, that the reintroduction to Day Lewis' poetry will not be. For he is the ideal Poet Laureate in his achievement—the ritual voice of a culture in its throes.

CONTENTS

Preface
Chronology
1. Poet Amid the Ideologies   17
2. The Crisis of Transition   39
3. The Poetics of Action   58
4. The End of Ideology   75
5. Journey from the Frontier   95
6. The Lyric Impulse   116
7. The Poetics of Hope   131
Notes and References   147
Selected Bibliography   151
Index   159

CHRONOLOGY

1904   Cecil Day-Lewis born April 27, in Ballintupper, Ireland; the only child of the Reverend C. Day-Lewis and Kathleen Blake Squires, a collateral descendant of Oliver Goldsmith.

1908   Mother died after the family had moved to England.

1917   Entered Sherborne School.

1923   Went up to Wadham College, Oxford.

1925   *Beechen Vigil*, his first book of poems, published at his own expense.

1927   Co-edited with Wystan Hugh Auden, *Oxford Poetry, 1927.* Came down from Oxford with a low fourth in Greats (classics).

1927–   Taught at Summer Fields preparatory school in North Oxford.

1928   *Country Comets,* a second book of juvenilia, published. Married Constance Mary King, by whom he would have two children.

1928–   Taught at Larchfield School, Helensburgh, Scotland, where he
1930   was succeeded in 1930 by Auden.

1929   *Transitional Poem,* his first substantial series poem.

1930–   Taught at Cheltenham public school.
1935

1931   *From Feathers to Iron,* a sequence of poems ostensibly based on the poet's emotional experience during the months before the birth of his first child.

1933   *The Magnetic Mountain.* First public linking of Day Lewis with the Auden Group in Michael Roberts' *New Signatures.*

1934   *A Hope for Poetry,* his first book of criticism.

1935   *A Time to Dance.* Under the pseudonym of Nicholas Blake, he published the first of many detective stories, *A Question of Proof.* Also, his *Collected Poems 1929-33* published.

1936   Verse play, *Noah and the Waters;* his first straight novel, *The Friendly Tree.*

1937   A second novel, *Starting Point.* Father died.

1938   *Overtures to Death.*

1939   *Child of Misfortune,* his third and final straight novel.

1940   *Poems in Wartime.*

1941   Translation of *The Georgics of Virgil.*

1943   *Word Over All,* which included the poems of *Poems in Wartime.*

1946–   Clark Lecturer at Trinity College, Cambridge.
1947

1947   *The Poetic Image,* the Clark Lectures for 1946.

1948   *Poems 1943-1947; Collected Poems 1929-1936.*

1951   Appointed Professor of Poetry at Oxford. Divorced from Mary King; married Jill Balcon.

1952   Translation of *The Aeneid of Virgil.*

1954   *Collected Poems 1954.*

1957   *Pegasus and Other Poems.*

1962   *The Gate and Other Poems.*

1965   *The Room and other poems;* a book of criticism, *The Lyric Impulse,* his Charles Eliot Norton lectures given at Harvard University in 1964–65.

1968   Appointed Poet Laureate of England, succeeding the late John Masefield, by Queen Elizabeth II.

CHAPTER 1

Poet Amid the Ideologies

F OR MORE than forty years, Cecil Day Lewis has been one of England's notable men of letters: poet, critic, and novelist; writer of detective stories; of children's books; Clark Lecturer at Cambridge; holder of the Oxford Chair of Poetry and Harvard University's Charles Eliot Norton lectureship. Now, decades after he earned his reputation as one of three radical young poets who were turning the course of English poetry away from a decadent and dying tradition toward a new, committed, futuristic style, he has become England's Poet Laureate and, in effect, the incarnation of the very establishment whose imminent death he had celebrated. Until his nomination to the Laureateship, Day Lewis' reputation and influence as a poet had suffered a steady decline from that time in the early 1930's when, along with W. H. Auden and Stephen Spender, he appeared to be a startlingly original voice whose work augured a radical discontinuity in the direction of modern poetry—and a return, as it were, of poetry to the middle, collective voice of the citizen in search of a just society. From the plateau of his recent eminence, it is difficult to recognize the young radical; just as it is difficult to recall that Day Lewis once challenged Auden, if only for a very brief time, as the most promising young poet of his age. Crowned by history, he and his poetry have been the victims of history's own radical perturbations.

I *The "Auden Group"*

Literary history has come to consider Day Lewis almost exclusively in terms of his association with Auden and Spender, as a member of the so-called Auden Group. And while the group image, as we shall see, overstates the actual homogeneity of the three poets and detracts from the individual talent of each (in particular, Auden's), the tendency to associate Day Lewis with a collective point of view and an impersonal poetry reveals a crucial truth about his work. From the

"Auden Group" to the Poet Laureateship, Day Lewis has sought in poetry to realize the self, or to discover a self, through self-effacement. His political and his personal poetry alike are of a piece, in that each begins with the vision of the disintegration of the self as mirrored in the disintegration of society. At the heart of Day Lewis' poetry is the search for a new society and thus a new language of human relationships; for language is not simply the medium of a culture but its infrastructure, and the self, if it is not to disappear, must be reconstituted in that structure. The fact of Day Lewis' belonging, if only figuratively, to a school or "Group" of poetry at the very time he emerged as a significant poet may be taken as an index to his career.

The "history" of the "Auden Group" is not limited to the relations, or even the specific achievements, of its three most famous members who, as both Spender and Day Lewis have testified, were never all together in the same room until long after they had ceased to be anything like a school of poetry. Spender's memoirs of the time, in *World Within World,* are to date the single most important commentary on the significance of their relations; and, like Day Lewis in his autobiography, *The Buried Day,* Spender concerns himself mainly with establishing the differences of sensibility which eventually led the three in divergent poetic directions.[1] The one thing neither disputes, however, is the dominance of Auden as a personality and conscience and the manner in which Auden's intellectual curiosity and the passion of his commitments superintended the interests of all those associated with him. Day Lewis had met Auden during the 1926-27 school year at Oxford, and almost immediately, as he says in *The Buried Day,* he was moved by the younger man's vitality and dedication to poetry, a vitality which in its excesses ran to "dogmatism, . . . intellectual bossiness, and the tendency to try to run his friends' lives for them" (176). Though Auden's influence would be indelible on almost everything Day Lewis wrote in the next decade, the mark of that influence most often reveals the struggle Day Lewis had in accommodating Auden's refined powers of abstraction with his own intellectual laziness that defended itself against the need to understand his emotional turmoil as a manifestation of the philosophical schisms of the time.

The two young poets combined to collect and edit *Oxford Poetry, 1927,* for which they wrote the now-famous Preface, declaring their generation gap not only from their Georgian ancestors but from T. S. Eliot, whose authority they nonetheless acknowledged, and from the pessimism of wasteland poetry. It was this Preface, the first of many polemics declaring the advent of a new age and a new poetry, and the first mature books of Day Lewis (*Transitional Poem* [1929]) and Auden (*Poems* [1930]), which led to the identification of an emerging new radicalism and the making of the "Auden Group." In 1932, a young Cambridgean named Michael Roberts brought the three poets together for the first time in a single collection, and in his introduction he nominated them as a "Group."[2] "We presented the unusual spectacle of an Oxford movement compered by Cambridge," Day Lewis recalled in *The Buried Day* (217); for the sponsor at the Hogarth Press, John Lehmann, was also a Cambridge graduate—as, in fact, were several of the other poets in the collection—because in Roberts' view the poets were not an Oxford, but a social movement.

Besides Auden, Day Lewis, and Spender, the anthology included Julian Bell, a young Cambridgean and the son of Clive and Vanessa Bell and nephew of Virginia Woolf, whose politics were to the ideological far right of the Oxford poets; William Empson, better known as critic; Day Lewis' college friend, Rex Warner, a classicist and later a novelist; and several minor voices, such as A. J. S. Tessimond. Roberts' polemical introduction made a strong point of the particular alliance of the Oxford group, but his primary concern, as Day Lewis put it in his autobiography, was to establish a "shared basis of thought," a mutual preoccupation with a poetry declaring its commitment to a new social union and the reintegration of the private, romantic will into the solidarity of a "system" (217). Poetry, Roberts argued, had to evoke this solidarity, by showing the possibility of man's subjectively integrating himself with the atomism of the technological state in a way analogous to the rustic's accommodation of an alien nature into his folkways: "Many poets have tried in recent years to use the material presented by modern civilisation, but they have only succeeded in presenting, as Mr. Tessimond does very precisely in 'La Marche des Machines,' a single sketch, an image or sequence of images, of something which is of itself beautiful. Mr. Auden's *Poems* and Mr. Day Lewis's *From Feathers to Iron* were, I think, the first books in which imagery taken from contemporary life consistently appeared as the natural and spontaneous expression of the poet's thought and feeling."[3] Roberts could thus ignore the classical opposites of political Right and Left because all the poets in his anthology were searching for the higher integration of the self into a coherent culture which transcended politics, a "system" in which the values of yoeman and poet, or proletarian and intellectual, were touched by a common purpose and connected by a common language. It involved him in a number of paradoxes which could be resolved only in the vision of an ideal future tied to an ideal (pastoral, and hence imaginary) past. Such futures, coherent and harmonious as they must be, could only be imaged in the coherent structures of poetry, in a new language:

The writers in this book have learned to accept the fact that progress is illusory, and yet to believe that the game is worth playing; to believe that the alleviation of suffering is good even though it merely makes possible new sensitiveness and therefore new suffering; to believe that their own standards are no more absolute than those of other people, and yet to be prepared to defend and to suffer for their own standards; to think of the world, for scientific purposes, in terms which make it appear deterministic, and yet to know that a human action may be unpredictable from scientific laws, a new creation.

These are not really logical problems at all; they are aspects of an emotional discord which can be resolved neither by reasoning nor by action, but only by a new harmonisation such as that which may be brought about by a work of art. The fact that each of the writers of this book has solved this problem in his own way without recourse to any external system of religious belief therefore opens up new poetic possibilities.[4]

The possibilities are, quite clearly, embodied in the poetic reconstitution of language, wherein is reconciled the romantic dualisms which generated the paradoxes of the free and determined self. The harmonizations discovered in poetry, in the new language, manifest the universal subject—the community of man. The single self is not free, but man is:

It is important that the recognition of the importance of others should sometimes lead to what appears to be the essence of the communist attitude: the recognition that oneself is no more important than a flower in a field; that it may be good to sacrifice one's own welfare that others may benefit; to plough in this year's crop so that next year's may benefit: the return is certain, what matter who receives it.

This impersonality comes not from extreme detachment but from solidarity with others. It is nearer to the Greek conception of good citizenship than to the stoical austerity of recent verse. . . .[5]

In a state of perfect communication, there is no private self or isolated subject. The subject exists only in relation to other subjects; the romantic self is sacrificed to the other, literally plowed back into the communal ground. The man who gives himself to the collective building of the new state and the poet who sacrifices his private emotions to the poem that renders those emotions impersonal are the architects of a new "solidarity." Solidarity and art are synonymous—a wholeness or coherence, a system with a center restored, in which Man replaces God.

Revolutionary poetry, as Stephen Spender wrote in Roberts' second anthology, *New Country,* might very well be "counter-revolutionary": "Poetry is a function of language, it records the changing uses of words and fixes their meaning, it preserves certain words in their pure and historic meaning, it saves the language from degenerating into looseness. Poetry also is a function of our emotional life . . . it is the language of moments in which we see ourselves or other people in our or their true relation to humanity or to nature. Poetry is certainly 'counter-revolutionary' in the sense that it contains an element of pity."[6] Poetry, that is, is nostalgic for an original order; the solidarity of language manifests a social solidarity. It also implies a sacrifice of the individual self as subject. The need of these poets for an impersonal poetry, while it derives theoretically from the argument set forth by Eliot in "Tradition and the Individual Talent," testifies in fact to another view toward history. Their ideal past, unlike Eliot's, was not the tradition as embodied in the venerable institutions—of Church, Crown, literature—but a time that, figuratively at least, antedates history and its time-haunted systems. They sought a *time* of some pastoral ideal, in which man's elementary relations to others and to nature were realized in coherent communities. Thus the Marxist future, with its ideal of a retrieved unity, became for them a kind of pastoral vision—the past recoverable in the future. Their occasional return to archaic form (the ballad and its recall of the oral tradition; Anglo-Saxon patterns) suggests the essentially counterrevolutionary thrust of a poetry that seeks to transcend the history of progress and its progressive dualisms.

The demand that poetry serve to integrate man's timeless emotional needs with the alien and alienating reality of the technological state must be seen, then, not as a sentimental attempt to adjust to modern reality, but as an attempt to incorporate into their new language the energy that could thrust them toward that ideal future. Technology harnessed the means to transcend itself. The modern evil was inertia. To go forward, however, they had to go back, to simplify, and to subordinate the self to the group. Many of them had learned this during their years in the public schools, when the dreaded threat of authority forced a retreat into clannishness, secret societies, and the like—groups with their own private language and codes. The lessons of twentieth-century history, as Stephen Spender observed, were indelibly written on their sensibilities before it was possible to consider these lessons intellectually or ideologically:

It can be seen now that the political preoccupations of the 1930's writers were part of a wider movement, though on the surface the directions of this movement were often opposed to one another. The general movement—more important than differences of politics and even of belief—was away from the extremes of individual vision towards the generally shared vision of some orthodoxy. The direction might be reactionary or it might be revolutionary, it might be religious or it might be materialist. But its depths were a shift away from personal originality towards the generalized tradition, from isolation within society towards points of view accepted by social groups, if not by the whole society.[7]

As Day Lewis' poetry makes evident, this movement also generates a crisis of identity; for to be creative the poet must lose himself. The problem of his freedom was a metaphysical before it was a political problem.

II   *The Buried Day Lewis*

Day Lewis was born in Ballintupper, Queens County, Ireland, on April 4, 1904, the only son of a curate of the Church of Ireland. The family moved shortly thereafter to England where the mother was soon to die, leaving the young boy of four to be reared by a maiden aunt and by a father whom he later described as excessively demanding and excessively loving. The obsessive themes of Day Lewis' poetry—the divided self, the transience of things and especially the tenuousness of human relationships, the lack of personal identity, the repeated departures from one security (usually a home) and the journey toward another, the discontinuity of present and past, the urgency of love and community—are all locatable, he points out in *Buried Day,* in the varieties of shock attendant upon his mother's sudden absence from his life (24). His early loss, however, is less significant as a particular psychological cause of his crisis of identity than as symptom of a generational problem. It left him a "curate's child" under the direct eye of the "curate" who was more than anything else the Victorian father. Day Lewis' early family life is, therefore, a metaphor of his generation's history.

But the young Day Lewis was not suddenly cast from a house of love and directly exposed to an authoritarian world; on the contrary, he came under the powerful emotional sway of a father who, as he later analyzed it, had a vigorous gift of love but was egregiously demanding of others. The father's sudden shift of egotistical affections from wife to son was apparently as trying for the young man as the uprooting of basic securities caused by his mother's death. Day Lewis' memoirs read like a Freudian textbook—especially as regards his professed hero worship of his father which was to turn into a lifelong tension and finally into almost total estrangement (see *Buried Day,* 21). The consequences of his loss of a mother, however, were not immediate; they appeared over a long period of time. The "abnormal tension" between father and son, as Day Lewis later called it, was the result of a strong bond between the two that lacked ultimately a strong maternal catalyst; and Day Lewis later identified his own creative urge as a feminine energy constantly threatened by masculine reason. His later indulgence of the Lawrencean mystique of the feminine has its roots here.

This personal history is not, of course, unique, but the particular admixture of an emotionally demanding clergyman-father and the substitute of an admired but evidently weak aunt for the mother that Day Lewis never really knew obviously had a profound impact on a sensitive young boy. Day Lewis remarks in *Buried Day*, for instance, on his reluctance to grow up, on his early passivity, and on his struggle to turn back into the memory of old securities (21). But the convulsive, as well as the idyllic, periods of his early years (the latter are almost always related to summer vacations with his aunt) paralleled historical events which had much the same impact. Educated at Sherborne School, where he enrolled in the last years of World War I, he entered Wadham College, Oxford, in 1923, ostensibly to read classics. "University life in 1923," he reflected in *The Buried Day*, "retained a certain Edwardian opulence and leisure" (159); but it afforded him crucial access to a world unanticipated by his previous life. Oxford was society, sport, and sophistication; but it was also an intellectually curious society—and, above all, it was a world at times as acutely aware of the immediate as of the remote past.

The Oxford which Day Lewis entered was sensitive to what the war had meant, even though it retained something of the Georgian aura of refined innocence which could ignore the more brutal shocks of history. Day Lewis' years there, especially after he came under the intellectual influence of Charles Fenby and Rex Warner, and after his meeting Auden, were a steady progress away from the cherished idyls of a prewar (both literally and figuratively, adolescent) world toward involvement in a society from which every security seemed to have disappeared. The progress implied a forfeiture of the nostalgic past and a recognition of the inevitability of some new world to come. In other words, his education heralded the past, celebrated the future, but made him uneasily aware of the incompleteness of the present. Everything reduced itself to the child's first sense of alienation and loss of identity and to his eagerness to regain for his generation something analogous to the old social order.

Stephen Spender has given eloquent testimony of the trials his generation endured in maturing amid the rationalizations and the hypocrisies of elders. "My parents and the servants talked of prewar days, as poets sing of a Golden Age," he says in *World Within World.* "The war had knocked the ball-room floor from under middle-class English life. . . . We were aware of the gulf but not of any new values to replace old supports. What was new seemed negative."[8] The new negativism he speaks of was England's version of the "lost generation" or the "jazz age"—the post-wasteland world, a world which had lost its teleological center and thus its future directions. Michael Roberts offers a similar reminiscence of his generation's historical innocence: "To me, 'pre-war' means only one sunny market day at Sturminister Newton, the day I boldly bought a goat for 1s. 9d. and then, shelving all transport problems . . . and postponing announcement to my father, went into the country. . . ."[9]

This sense of World War I as an absolute break with the past was intoned throughout the 1930's even in the leftist journals. The 1920's were considered historically inevitable because of the war; indeed, even the tougher British intellectuals tended to see the war as an historical watershed at which point a mythical, pastoral world had been fragmented into an industrial, technological one. What is surprising is how easily the intellectual leftists of the 1930's could disregard the whole history of the Industrial Revolution and also the moral and social dislocations of the Victorian and Edwardian periods—surprising until we reflect that the war coincided with their own transition from youth to manhood, their abrupt journey out of Georgian innocence into modern guilt. It is almost certainly true, as John Strachey indicated in the *Left Review* in 1934, that the growth of Marxism in England was more the result of a moral than of an economic convulsion in the society; it was the absolute disillusionment of a generation whose fall from innocence had been dramatically manifest in history:

My generation of Englishmen . . . remembers the pre-war world, but remembers it as a vision of childhood; and for a well-circumstanced English child what a golden age of peace, calm, plenty, and security it was! . . . For me the "pre-war" evokes always a memory of midsummer afternoons.

. . . . .

My generation of Englishmen became conscious of the break-up of our world, not by realizing that its economic foundations were shattered, but by a sudden and bewildering loss of faith in the whole moral, religious, and social ideology we had inherited. And this is why our revolt came first of all in those fields.[10]

Despite events like the General Strike of 1926, which moved numbers of university students to activism (Day Lewis dramatized his own ambiguous allegiances with the strikers in a novel he published in 1937, *Starting-Point*)—and despite evident flaws in the social fabric of the 1920's, there was little direct awareness among these poets that the economic foundations of immediate postwar England were insecure. The Oxford poets gave little thought to economics as such; and, even in the 1930's, when they had in Day Lewis' words "mugged-up" their Marx, they simply became more aware of the economic basis of society and hence of the economic forces attendant upon history, poetry, and the poet. In fact, Day Lewis seems to have first become alerted to the crisis as it was manifest in literature (the crisis of language) rather than in society. Young intellectuals like Fenby and Warner made him aware of the age's need for a coherent philosophy (a "system") and hence of its lack of one. What intellectual ferment there was at Oxford directed itself at the dilemma posed by Eliot's anatomy of the present metaphysical and hence spiritual crisis. Warner, evidently, introduced a somewhat reluctant Day Lewis to the complexities and contradictions of the great philosophical systems; but, Day Lewis admitted in *Buried Day*, he became lost in their mutually attractive counterclaims (166-67). The experience no doubt was fundamental to his development as a poet, particularly to his abrupt change from the bucolic verse he was writing during his first years at Oxford to the intellectual analysis of *Transitional Poem.*

Auden's catholic interest had the similarly healthy effect of pointing out that poetry did not exclude intellect and that man's relation to nature was not pastoral. Auden's wide intellectual net made it evident that, if a culture were disintegrating, the symptoms would be present in every strand of its life. His readings in psychology, natural science, religion, and philosophy prepared him to see the next great apocalpytic system, Marxism, not as an exclusively economic theory of history but as a concept that claimed to attend to the moral whole. Even before the economic dislocations of the late 1920's and early 1930's made a social conscience *de rigueur,* Auden was cautioning his peers about poetry's involvement in social transition. The members of the "Auden Group" came to Marxism not because of its undeniable truth but because it was the one system which directed itself at all the ills of society. In other words, they came to Marxism through attending to the crisis in literature—one which for them touched simultaneously on the moral, psychological, philosophical, religious, and social realities—while, for the Marxist intellectual, literature tended to derive it assumptions and values from an economic and social determinism rather than create those values. These poets regarded literature as a force for changing society (by first altering its emotional core—the change of heart), but the Marxist theoreticians (excepting possibly Trotsky) considered literature to be the effect of historical change. What these poets really needed was some continuation of the poet's traditional role in his culture's life in order to counteract Eliot's negativism and his diminishment of the poet's force in the historical process; but like Eliot and the Marxists they regarded the Romantic egocentrism as the fundamental threat to the social order. And so they came to agree that fundamentally history or tradition must precede and direct the individual talent.

This summation of the situation oversimplifies the impact of Oxford on Day Lewis—but the Oxford years were ones of emotional and intellectual revolt. They were also a time of fortunately concentrated experience during which the lengthier years of his adolescence and his estrangement from his father were brought into focus as symptomatic of a cultural, not simply a personal, revolution. When Day Lewis matriculated at Wadham, he brought with him the sensibility of a Georgian world, one reinforced by his own essentially rural upbringing and by the impact of growing up as the "curate's child." The two books of poems written during his undergraduate years, *Beechen Vigil* (1925) and *Country Comets* (1928), are unblushingly the harvest of this Georgian milieu. Oxford could not really take the country out of the boy, but it could start him reflecting on the meaning of that world which had seemed to curry to his sensual needs without satisfying any of them. And *Country Comets,* which was not published until after he left Oxford, contains some residual tones of doubt about nature's order and her ministrations to man. Nature, as he later reflected, was something he had to learn to feel; he did not embrace her naturally.

These early books of poems were the product of his awakening to his own sensual nature, to the other, and hence to love—a phenomenon he returned to again and again in his poetry and fiction of the 1930's, but he superimposed his emotional awakening upon the myth of social revolution. In the Preface to *Oxford Poetry, 1927,* written in collaboration with Auden, and then in *Transitional Poem,* some of which had appeared in the earlier anthology, Day Lewis first revealed the analytical spirit which later manifested itself in dialectical poetics. Nature, in these poems, lost her magic and became the self's nonhuman antithesis but remained the immediate ground of being. The perennial philosophical question of mind's relation to matter was easily extended into that of the poet's relation to society. The departure from his adolescent Georgian world was socially analogous to the metaphysical death of God; all coherence disappeared with it, leaving mind rootless, a nothingness, disembodied. Thus, the divided self.

In fact, Auden's earliest influence on Day Lewis' thinking appeared to lie precisely in his calculatedly ambiguous view of the relation of mind and matter; for Auden's early flirtations with Freud and with the aberrant psychologies of Georg Groddeck and Homer Lane taught him to attach psychic illness to the failure of mind to dominate matter or, oppositely, to the hubris of will's "negative inversion." Indeed, this is the issue of the modern world as Day Lewis first encountered it. In an age of analysis, he had to affirm the syncretic powers of the poet. Oxford, which as he said in *Buried Day* taught the serious youth the wisdom of the lighter touch (179), nevertheless prepared him for commitment. It is indicative that his first major poem emerged from his investigations of what role the poet might, and must, play in the modern world; for Day Lewis' immediate heritage from the past was an image of disorder. The question was whether the poet could, or must, manage a new synthesis—or build a new "system" out of the fragments of old ones—since synthesis, rather than analysis, was the poet's traditional function. The new synthesis, whatever else it might be, must incorporate the old order, and hence be true to tradition and its language. Or better, the deconstruction of an old system can only be made in the language of that system, since the new world and its language do not exist. The poet like the synthetic philosopher is dedicated to building his new world out of the fragments of the old one. In this sense alone could the "tetragonal/Pure symmetry of brain" (*Collected Poems,* 13) be a manifestation not of the private will but of the "collective consciousness," and the poet be both the agent and the instrument of the dialectical will of history.

III   *Between Lawrence and Marx*

Long before Marxism became a part of Day Lewis' thinking, D. H. Lawrence and Freud had already claimed his allegiance—Lawrence more so than Freud, and both largely because of Auden. In *The Buried Day*, Day Lewis has remarked how Lawrence "got mixed into my Marxism" because each indicted a "system" (capitalism) which prevented the "full flowering of individual personality" and hence "affected the relationship between man and woman, poisoning it with false idealism that encouraged only the self-conscious and cerebral sides of our nature" (210). The impact of economic turbulence on individual relationships was the subject of Day Lewis' three legitimate novels written in the mid-1930's, though in them he could follow neither the strict Marxian nor the rigid Lawrencean line; and the blurring of the two only reflected the hopeless mixture of two irreconcilable philosophies. The full flowering of the individual personality implied for Day Lewis the submission of the private will to the wholeness of the love relationship and thus an escape from the "negative inversion" of the will. "Lawrence spent half his life dinning that into our ears," Day Lewis wrote in *A Hope for Poetry* (44).

Auden alone, clearly, could reconcile Lawrence and Freud, or Lawrence and Marx—could reconcile antithetical ideologies and faiths not by being true to them but by being true to himself. "Thought's chameleon" was Day Lewis' apt phrase for Auden in *Transitional Poem* (Collected Poems, 21)—he whose "Single mind copes with split intelligence,/Breeding a piebald strain of truth and nonsense." Auden's genius for abstraction, his ability to generalize out compatible elements in alien philosophies, his way of maintaining simultaneously incoherent and inconsistent points of view, yet managing somehow to synthesize all into a poem without wholly partisan commitments—this quality was a genius which Day Lewis lacked. And so Auden's flirtations with Lawrence, Freud, and Marx tended more to accentuate the impossibility of reconciliation and to underscore the artifice of his attempt at a large synthesis. For his poetics were ultimately not an attempt to reduce an atomistic world of ideas to an essential harmony; on the contrary, they are a poetics of extraction, of a deliberately coherent comic point of view derived from a body of antithetical ideologies and leavened with a sense of humor that places all such reductive exercises of the human mind into problematic (yet viable) perspective. Auden's game theory of art saves him from demanding ultimate truth of poetry, just as it saves his poetry from pretending to render that truth. Auden's is the perspective of the human "mean"—and the pun is clear enough.

Auden, that is, achieved impersonality and yet an authentically individual poetic style precisely because of his ability to identify with alien modes of thought and points of view without embracing any one of them as a solution of the existential dilemma. (In this respect he was consistent in his later shift of allegiance to a Kierkegaardian ethic and poetics.) The key to Day Lewis' early poetics, on the other hand, lies in his tireless search for a system that confirms impersonality. He interpreted the will's "negative inversion" not like Auden as the distortions of an aggressive personal *id* (or *It*, to be consistent with Groddeck's term) which leads to an imbalance between need and desire and hence to a self-destroying guilt, but as the Lawrencean version of modern man's death wish. For Auden, the assertion of the individual will was a force that could only have destructive consequences; but it was a positive force. For Day Lewis, such an assertion was thoroughly negative (not a negative inversion, or tautologically, a force which when inverted had negative or destructive consequences). Day Lewis completely accepted the Lawrencean view, especially Lawrence's faith in the transcending synthesis of emotional relationships; but Day Lewis could find no satisfactory hope in Lawrence's vision for practical alleviation of present social chaos. Moreover, Day Lewis distrusted Lawrence's romanticism, presumably because it reflected so much light on his own. And so he wandered between dream and reality, hope and despair, faith in spirit and submission to matter—between, that is, Lawrence and Marx, but he rested with neither of them.

Auden's intellectualism had its ambiguous impact on Day Lewis' style. Auden's poetry moves from idea to reality—or it moves from an experience that is largely intellectual to a contemplation of ideas which admits their rich and often comic impingements upon life. Life renders the idea problematic, throwing it into comic relief. For Auden language is a human mean, and logos an illusion. Day Lewis' natural mode was lyrical; his primary thematic concerns are with the harmony of the emotional life. His attempt in *Transitional Poem* not only to impose the "tetragonal/ Pure symmetry of brain" on modern chaos but to contemplate the implications of that urgent necessity (in a poem presumably both analytic and synthetic) had stylistic consequences that set his art in conflict with his sensibility. His development in the 1930's and early 1940's can be said, in effect, to have altered the ratio of idea to experience in his poetry but not to have changed his basic theme: the divided self, in which emotion and reason are at odds. Even as he moved more and more toward a public and a committed poetry, he was moved, as he later acknowledged, not by intellectual but by emotional convictions. His Marxism followed intimate exposure to the social injustice of the 1930's and not the mere reading of the *Communist Manifesto*. As more than one critic has attested, Day Lewis, of all the Auden Group, is the most attentive to the actual details of his immediate world, and hence he should have been the most authentic Marxist poet—the recorder of the material process of history in revolution.

But it was Auden, whose commitments were neither intellectually nor emotionally absolute, who wrote the radical poetry—who caught the living tensions of man in the midst of psychological, moral, and social transition. In contrast to Auden, the distracting quality of Day Lewis' work throughout the 1930's is its schizophrenic dedication now to social change, now to emotional conservatism, which manifests itself in poems like *From Feathers to Iron* in a technological language used to evoke basic emotional responses to change and death. As a result the poet's private reaction to the forthcoming birth of his first child, and the possibility of his wife's death in childbirth, becomes a metaphor for the anxieties of social revolution and the psychic consequences of experiencing the advent of a new society. The crux of his dilemma, clearly, is that he is at once creator-father and the sacrificial figure to this new world, this future family. The emotional and the intellectual are never successfully reconciled in the mythic pattern of the journey to some new country—precisely because the subject is not political or prophetic but personal.

Day Lewis' experiments in the use of a technological imagery, following Auden's lead, did not allow for the necessary irony with which Auden leavened his intellectual game. We are always conscious of the poem's two distinct levels but too seldom of their appropriate parallel. For all Day Lewis' good faith in attending to the social crisis, the emotional center of his poetry remained in his struggle with his own inner conflict, with his own "divided heart" as he later put it (*Buried Day*, 212). His search for a myth or a "system" by which to order experience and to make history coherent was, as it developed, his way of escaping from the labyrinth of his own internal conflict—of turning his inner life outward into the social sphere. His was an attempt to escape the romantic will, to transcend the self in impersonality; but he did so by asserting that man's only method of self-transcendence lay in creation—begetting children, new societies, or poems—and thereby in sacrificing the private self to the future of community and order.

When Day Lewis discovered and abandoned Marx within a few short years, his poetry did not suffer any radical changes in theme or emphasis—only certain stylistic ones. After leaving the university in 1927, he began teaching at Summer Fields in Oxford. A year later he moved to Larchfield School, Helensburgh, Scotland; two years later, he joined the Cheltenham public school where he remained until 1936 when he got into trouble with authorities over a combination of difficulties: political activities and the publication of his first detective novel. He was married (to Constance Mary King) shortly after the move from Summer Fields to Larchfield, and for a brief time at the end of his teaching career he joined the Communist party. But, for most of the eight years—those in which he wrote nearly all the poetry on which his reputation rests—he worked his art into the rhythms of an essentially domestic and rural life. The ideological dimension of his early poems were deliberate intellectual extensions of personal themes, but the two are not always fused to good effect.

From Feathers to Iron is the most distinguished product of his attempt to reconcile private and public experience; and it is a most ambivalent success at best. But in *The Magnetic Mountain,* which followed two years later, Day Lewis turned almost exclusively to ideology as prophecy; he used Marxian theory to project a futuristic vision so compelling that all the anxieties attendant upon leaving the old world could be ignored. Yet, like the earlier sequence of poems, this poem was not so much visionary and prophetic as a statement of private conviction. For both poems reveal a Lawrencean bias: that any move toward a new society, and even any new society itself, is immanent in the life will, the creative impulse. Day Lewis' new worlds always appeared as strangely like some idyllic old ones—centered upon the family, bound by the force of self-sacrificing love, and grounded in some pastoral retreat—all as perfect as a poem. When Day Lewis looked outward to his industrial world and attempted to naturalize its language, he really wanted to transform it back into some kind of pastoral myth, except that common sense told him not to do so. So his projected new world—his magnetic mountain—remained unvisualized; it was evoked in terms at once contemporary and pastoral, futuristic and nostalgic.

When Day Lewis eventually contemplated the realities of social evolution in the context of dialectical materialism, he had lost the sense of mystery that lay in his earlier "faith" of the future—a faith nurtured by his own sensual and moral involvement in marriage and family and by his intense commitment to poetry, that ultimate realization of the creative will. The priority of personal feeling to ideology marked him, in Christopher Caudwell's terms, as an unremitting bourgeois radical who was divided against himself. The pseudo-dramatic debates of *The Magnetic Mountain* painfully confirm Caudwell's assessment of Day Lewis's ties with the old society. Indeed, his ultimate concern was in finding a society safe for poetry.

"The positive beliefs I was moving towards in the earlier Thirties," he has said retrospectively in *Buried Day*, "did not ramify from any central faith; they were rather, substitutes for a faith, heterogeneous ideas which served to plug 'the hollow in the breast where God should be. '" (209). His communism, he added, "had a religious quality. It was also romantic, and in more ways than one" (209—10). We need to be even more circumspect than that as regards the admixture of faith and ideology in the 1930's, but there is no gainsaying the poets' awareness of the apocalyptic potential of Marxism and their need for a "system" that would guarantee them a future, and thus a creative identity. Auden's brilliance at the abstractive reduction of new ideas into mythic patterns is in its way complementary to Day Lewis' tendency to see human events as epical or mythical movements, acted out by figures remotely suggesting a morality play—heroes, underdogs, and enemies.

Day Lewis even describes in *Buried Day* his own joining of the Communist party as the logical end of a series of passionate commitments, rather than as the passionate end of a series of logical choices: "What attracted me most . . . in the Communist philosophy was the concept that we discover reality by acting upon it, not thinking about it" (212). The need for a poetry of action—a poetry that would move its audience to a "change of heart"—was urgent not simply because the era called for revolution, but because it was necessary for the poet to assume once again his creative role at the cultural center. In the shift of social contexts to come, the poet had to renew his active role, not withdraw as in the 1920's into the refuge of art or cynicism or despair.

As Maurice Merleau-Ponty has observed, history cannot be absolutely determined for the Marxist if the revolution is not inevitable, which it is not; and hence man, to make the revolution, must be in a degree free;[11] thus the self is a product-producer, manifest in and manifesting the intersubjective reality that is society and history. The passionate catalyst of the poet's voice, Day Lewis allowed himself to hope, could rise in freedom more objectively than the Hegelian spirit to initiate a materialist revolution. Auden's "change of heart," because it began in the individual subject and moved outward to the intersubjective social life, was fundamentally anti-Marxist; but like the Marxists, Auden could not conceive of the individual subject apart from or prior to the community of subjects that made up a social group. Poetry might initiate a change of heart, then, not because it issued from the imagination of a private self, but because it was the desire of a cohesive group in the process of transforming and being transformed by language. Poetry was language undergoing transformation—and thus man changing.

Like the father in *From Feathers to Iron,* all futures begin with a vital human act; sex and the imagination are the progenitors of history, yet they are equally the products of history. Both poets and poems stand in the present looking forward and back—and thus are analogues of the myth of history. If Day Lewis' sense of how the poet could be at once a force in history and the impersonal instrument of historical force seems hazy, his conviction that he must assume both roles is not:

The tradition of poetry for the last hundred years has been developed by a dominating class, the bourgeoisie. Until the domination of that class is ended, revolutionary writers, whether bourgeois or workers, have to make the best of its tradition. A tradition cannot be created independently of the social framework,whatever variations on it may be achieved by individual writers. . . . A poetic tradition is the mould into which the poet sets his materials: to melt down these moulds and form new ones out of the mass needs nothing less intense than the flame of the achieved social revolution. Until we have that, the poet must use the traditional moulds and depend for originality on the material he puts into them.[12]

The place of the poet's act is, in effect, between two worlds; it is the present, where alone there is life and death, incessant creation and change. Poets are not, we note, architects of a future: neither are they prophets nor, more significantly, the instruments of some pure spirit. To return to the Hegelian metaphor, they are a part of the spirit without which matter is moribund. That spirit, the modern poet can only assume, lies in the desire of man; it is his innocence and his energy, his life will, not some transcendent Absolute. When Day Lewis turns to the proletariat, or the English yeoman, to celebrate goodness, vitality, or the life will, he turns, of course, to the people among whom he was reared; but he touches them with a mythic aura of innocence and vitality. Bearing within themselves the purity of some lost world, they desire a new one. In the same way, he turns the rural world into a garden of imagination, set against the iron city. The country is his metaphoric space of creation—a projection of his own innocence and purity when making poems and hence participating in the primal act of creation.

In other words, Day Lewis' poetry of action constantly threatens to turn in upon itself; for it is obsessively centered upon the question of creation. The issues surrounding that question are in part those posed by Eliot's traditionalism, in which creative self-consciousness demands a surrender of the individual to the cultural or institutional will and ultimately to the Divine Will. Or, to put it another way, tradition denies the role of self as creator, a denial made paradoxically in the very act of creating the poem which is an extension of the tradition. A poetry of action, a poetry bent on motivating by the very passion of its processes a change of heart, was the recourse not simply of poets who had developed a social conscience because they were witness to an unjust history, but of those who would preserve the crucial role of poetry itself as a creative force. The revolutionary poets of the 1930's stood resolutely in the middle; yet they found the kind of philosophical and meditative paralysis that afflicted their great predecessors. Yeats and Eliot, impossible. Having to take sides, they had to assume the role of actor, both in history and against history. Even in surrendering the individual self to the revolutionary will and process, they participated as a force in history. And their radical poems, especially Day Lewis' apparently political poems, are really about that role: the paradox of creating that which subsumes the creator. The lack of focus in those poems—their dependence on traditional forms or "moulds," yet their impatient search for a modern language; their often artless attempt to employ deeply personal experience as a metaphor or archetype for prescribed social changes, as in the incessant journeys—is in effect a blurring of the poet's role. They are poems intent on projecting the vision of a future, but their primary function is the deconstruction of a moribund present.

The real subject of these poems is themselves—the poet taking a double look at his role as at once the maker and the victim of history. The struggle toward impersonality—which manifests itself technically in a thoroughly metaphorical poetry wherein all analogies are horizontal and thrust themselves toward an ever receding future—only serves to call attention to the poet's self-transcending act in assuming his role. When he sacrifices his individual self to the role of poet and also to the inspirational force which not only preserves the immutable forms of the past but provokes changes of heart, he becomes more than a person. He becomes a part of the human will for rebirth, incarnating itself in the vision of a new society. But it is a society he can never realize actually, except that he possesses it in his own dream of self-transcendence manifest most intensely in the condition of love.

Critics have never failed to remark on the coterie quality of Auden's and Day Lewis' early poetry, especially its appeal to a private, intimate society of schoolboys who had their obscure language and codes of honor. This "clubby," yet obscure, society was, for Day Lewis at least, a metaphor for the beginning of a new society which incorporated, of course, the gestures of the old. The first vestiges of his new society, interestingly enough, is a group of poets—the small social group that Day Lewis conceived of in *A Hope for Poetry* (36–38) as bound together by love, mutual interests, a common language, and a common purpose. This society, like the schoolboy society of his and Auden's poems, is purified of human inertia; it is a group of creators, dedicated to a future society which they are vigorously making in the present. It is a society, that is, primarily dedicated to making poems—those *advents,* to use a term of the phenomenologists, of the future which are the ongoing processes of the present.

To state the intent all too simply, this small society which Day Lewis foresaw in *A Hope for Poetry* as the beginning of a new society of the future, this group which provides the metaphors of the public-school and boy-scout world of Auden's and Day Lewis' early poems—this society is something more than an attempt to rationalize the poet's need of tradition and his alienation from it. The societal ambition is a concealed, even self-concealed, assertion of the poet as sole creator in a materialistic world which had denied the purposiveness of creation and retreated into skepticism and the contingency of history. To say that these poems were about themselves, about the creative process, is not, therefore, to deny their authors' plea for impersonal creation. For to transcend the social self and become the poetic self was, as we have noted, to become one with the creative will itself—which these poets could no longer identify with something like the Hegelian Spirit but which they could identify as the self-transcending impulse of love in man.

To celebrate the creative self is to celebrate the superhuman; and, as Day Lewis would claim in his later books of criticism, long after the need to reconcile his poetics with Marxism and revolution had passed, every poem strives to confirm man's superhumanity. The poem, that is, is a reaching toward wholeness; hence it reaches beyond the individual to the "communal experience" (*Poetic Image,* 144). And the superhuman in man is just his ability to entertain the "illusion of completeness" or wholeness (145) and hence to live in his present the future and past. But that "wholeness" toward which man strives—that lifewill which mandates his immortality and his poems—is entertained only as an "illusion." Like Auden's repeated assertion of man's meanness, Day Lewis finds in man's urge toward wholeness the fullest recognition of his limitation—of Hegal's meaning that man is desire.

Poems, like *From Feathers to Iron*, which celebrate the transcendence of self in the creative act, must entertain the irony of its limitation in the same shock of recognition. Man makes a new society and a new poem by sacrificing his individual self. The moment of the creative act, the present, is thus at once a moment of self-transcendence and self-sacrifice—a reintegration of the divided self by making it communally whole. Creation is the act of love. But, of course, only the moment of the act, like sexual climax, is whole, both a beginning and an end. As Day Lewis revealed in *The Magnetic Mountain*, the ultimate consummation is always beyond; but, if man lives inside a coherent "system," he can live in the immediacy of his own future. Yet, as the 1930's wore on, and as the "magnetic mountain" seemed even more remote than attractive, Day Lewis had to confront the starker and more obvious end of man's quest for self-transcendence—death. His *Overtures to Death* (1938) appropriately ended a decade of faith, which we must now regard as not so much faith supported by ideology as faith based on the illusion of a future. Death, including the death of the self, is intrinsic to the continuity of things, and implicit in the desire for any new world.

IV *The Future of Illusions*

Communism's betrayals of the future, in the late 1930's, were for Day Lewis the ultimate failure of "system." But however intense his disillusionment, it was reflected only momentarily in his poetry, which was engaged with a more enduring despair. *Overtures to Death* signified the end of his belief in historical futures; after all, those "magnetic mountains" were ideals he had allowed himself to entertain only because he could endorse a faith in man's ability to change not only himself but also the processes of history. In retrospect, the poetry of those "future-fans" of the 1930's turns out to be a poetry of historical immediacy. After 1938, Day Lewis' poetry seems to become, therefore, more his own: it is less ambitious, more introspective, inevitably less topical, and more nostalgic. But the old preoccupations remain; indeed, their implications are even more apparent. Day Lewis' search in the 1930's for a tradition and a language—a "system" which preceded the self and confirmed it—was destined to fail because it was based on historical nostalgia. The collapse of the last ultimate "system" forced him to revaluate the tradition within which the poet works. And what he discovered was that tradition is the "illusion" of wholeness the poet holds to as he lives in the present and points himself toward the future. Tradition is a myth or totalization that attempts to answer man's desire; thus, poetry would become his myth.

In the past thirty years, Day Lewis has produced at least seven volumes of poetry, a book of memoirs, and three major books of criticism. He has remained an independent man of letters; and periodically he has returned to his first profession, teaching. But, as a poet, he has not significantly developed, even though he has, as it were, discovered his earlier self and what it meant for a young man of his generation to take poetry as a career. He has discovered, that is, the role of poetry in the human economy. As he has failed to be an original poet (he was that, perhaps, only for a brief time), he has found the true necessity of his vocation: poetry is a spiritual exercise in self-renewal and in self-transcendence, the method whereby the individual self survives in a world from which all systems had defected and only love was cohesive. In the illusory wholeness of the poem man possesses himself as timeless, at "home," and thus located in the interstices rather than the flow of history.

In a very obvious sense, Day Lewis' highly autobiographical poetry of the years following 1940 is a more convincing engagement of history than his earlier poetry of commitment. His search for his earlier self admits inexorable process in a way his futuristic poetry did not—for, ultimately, a faith in the consummations of "magnetic mountains" tempers the anxieties of the existential moment. Day Lewis' truest "political" poem was *From Feathers to Iron,* not *Transitional Poem* or the *Magnetic Mountain* which came just before and just after. *From Feathers to Iron,* hedged as it is with an elation and an optimism about the journey to a new world, is nevertheless centered in the contingency and anxiety of the present. Its subject, the ambiguities of creative action, is overlayed with historical, political, and ideological hints that tend to mitigate the personal dilemma; but the poem is nonetheless a true index of the personal as well as of the social crisis at the center of Day Lewis' art.

Dualism (the divided self) remained his theme. It translates itself into a variety of schisms, which provide Day Lewis with his own creative dialectic: the discontinuity of past and present, which is manifest in the alienation of the present generation; the schism of language, reflected everywhere in its connotative and denotative functions; the divided self, whose unconscious is at war with its conscious; the self's sense of its fall from wholeness into desire which was both creative and destructive.

For a while in the 1940's Day Lewis became a student of French post-Symbolist poetry, or at least of Paul Valéry, some of whose poems he translated. Apparently incapable of responding to the abstract intellectualism of Valéry, Day Lewis tended to translate the French poems into versions of English meditative verse. But he did not fail to grasp the modern urgency of Valéry's hope for poetry—the poem's "illusion of wholeness" and hence the poet's struggle through it to make himself whole again. Poetry as self-renewal—that is, in effect, the one theoretical preoccupation of Day Lewis' during the last three decades; but it has its precedent in his earlier journeys. His introspective, personal lyrics seem to betray his earlier theory of impersonality. But the poems of introspection (and, we hasten to add, Day Lewis' poems of reminiscence are not introspective in the Romantic sense) are attempts to refine out the person by way of discovering his whole self, which lies most purely in the commonness of his experience and in the most fundamental of his relationships.

Day Lewis may serve us today as a relevant example of the poet-in-history as opposed to the poet-on-Parnassus. He is one of the few instances we have of an artist whose work was catalyzed by ideology into being better than it might otherwise have been. But, if this is the case, it is so only because that ideology spoke emphatically to emotional truths he already held and enforced them as historically objective. Today, that objectivity appears less relevant, certainly less urgent, than it did in the 1930's, and poetry is less effective as a force that alters political and economic structures rather than being altered by them. Today we see not Marx in Day Lewis' early poetry but the perennial emotional food of a faith in telic order that affirms self-identity and man's creative role in history. For Day Lewis had discovered that man is language and thus is condemned to interpret himself repeatedly. He is condemned, that is, to seek his own origin and his own end because he is enmeshed in a network of relations that forever obscure origins and ends.

CHAPTER 2

The Crisis of Transition

WHEN Day Lewis arrived at Oxford, he was a rather naïve, sensitive young man. At Oxford, he became a poet, but not before he had written a good deal of verse that reflected more the limitations of his experience than his future talent. He went up to college from the fractured innocence of a public school, and he never outgrew the sense that the crucial acts of his life were dramatic changes of place: dislocations, journeys, abrupt transitions. These, in fact, became his recurrent metaphors.

He began as a poet of sensibility, though the sensibility of his two early books of poems appears to have been acquired somewhere between the losses and defections of love in his childhood and the literary education suffered by a young man in the full blush of Georgian England. Oxford and Auden quickly disabused him of the privilege of indulging in his own emotions. But no matter how Day Lewis developed or matured, adopted philosophical or ideological stances, all his future experience tended to adjust itself to the primacy of the emotions. For Day Lewis, the first crisis was last and always, and the first crisis, after one had acquired a self, was a transition which threatened one's identity.

I The Primacy of Environment

Transitional Poem appeared in 1929, as the ninth volume of the Hogarth Living Poets Series. Appropriately, it marked the advent of Day Lewis' maturity, both as man and as poet; for the poem is directed more to the future than to the past. That change, in fact, is its significance; the transition it explicitly announces is multileveled, and the poem exploits the "transitional" metaphor throughout. The poem was begun, evidently, well before the publication of *Country Comets* (1928), parts of it appearing in *Oxford Poetry, 1927,* which Day Lewis had edited jointly with Auden. It is a difficult (because personally obscure) and not altogether successful poem. But it is also one of the most revealing documents we have of the young poets who had to grow up to a new and alien postwar world, bereft of the kind of traditional consolations that had supported the dominant style of English poetry since the Victorian period. Yet, the poem is no less uncomfortable with the varieties of experiment provoked by postwar disillusionment.

Characteristically, *Transitional Poem* evinces a great deal of the moral and social collapse which obsessed English poetry of the 1920's and indicates the kind of self-conscious dependence upon the new from which a poetic style had almost literally to be contrived. Its literary ancestors are not really, as it may first appear, the Victorians and Georgians (who provided the style for Day Lewis' first two volumes), but were derived from the eclectic fragments of an undergraduate education and from the directions pointed by Eliot, through Auden, to the enduring, timeless (and ironically, personal) tradition any individual talent might share. That it was Auden, along with Rex Warner, who introduced Day Lewis to the new poetry (of Eliot, of war poets like Wilfred Owen, of Hopkins) there is little doubt. What is important, however, is the manner of his response—or better, his way of absorbing what was urgently relevant to his needs.

Transitional Poem is pastiche, the only style available to the poet who must necessarily sweep away the failed past. But pastiche is, precisely, the stamp of the individual talent: the unique voice emerging from the fragments of its knowledge and manifesting itself in the order, only partly its own, it imposes upon that knowledge. If its knowledge is of the past, of tradition, Day Lewis' use of it is committed to the present. He did not have, as we have observed, as unique a talent as Auden for assimilating alien ideas and, hence, for synthesizing pastiche into a personal style. Day Lewis' gropings for a style, in fact, make him a mirror to a generation that, having lost its trust in the past, held little hope for the future. Yet, in the face of despair it had to will a future.

Transitional Poem labors under intellectual pretensions. They are not, however, like Auden's, pretensions of genius; but are, instead, the bumptiousness of a confused young man who stubbornly refuses to be submerged in confusion. Of all Day Lewis' poems, this one is the most typical of his real talent and the most revealing also of what he had to ask of poetry. For him, as for Robert Frost, poetry had to be some kind of clarification of life; the act of poetry is Day Lewis' necessary mode of escape from subjectivity, a way through and out of the crisis of self-consciousness to some momentary stay against confusion. Like Valéry, with whom Day Lewis later discovered an affinity, he identified the process of the poem as that of making (or re-creating) oneself—in his particular instance, of relating the present self to the earlier buried self (adult guilt to the child's innocence) and, thereby, of making oneself whole again. Poetry's perfection—or its "illusion" of manifest wholeness—is a recurrent theme of his criticism.

Transition, then, means simultaneously a number of things in this poem; and the purpose of the poem is to reconcile all its meanings in the experience of oneself. Principally, the transition is from youth to manhood and, hence, from innocence to guilt; from dependence to responsibility; from isolation to community; and thus from egotism to love. On one level, the poem records this movement as an awakening of the sexual self, bespeaking the urgency of a binding, unifying interpersonal relationship. Love bridges the abyss that has isolated the self in self-consciousness—that fall, as the poem explicitly treats it, which occurs in adolescence, cutting off the self from the communal securities of its youth and leaving it with the desire for some new community. The transition is thus a painful but necessary severing from the past, from home and tradition, and from all that they imply.

The game and gang motifs (the boy-scout atmosphere) so ably manipulated by Auden and imitated by Day Lewis in their earliest poems must be seen, even by one critically indisposed toward their literary propriety, as a serious attempt to reinvoke the lost social order without which the poet, as Eliot cautioned, could not function in his accustomed role. Or rather, they are attempts, at once ironic and serious, to imitate the present crisis, in which the younger poets must lead the way from the dying culture to the frontiers of a new one, maintaining in their own little circle the essential seeds of communal order from which the new world would grow. The difference between Auden and Day Lewis was, by and large, Auden's humor, his ironic indisposition to allow seriousness to overwhelm his good sense of esthetic decorum or to exceed the intrinsic limits of poetry.

The metaphysical necessity of *Transitional Poem* urges a new poetics and a new style. In the Preface to *Oxford Poetry, 1927*, Auden and Day Lewis had issued a manifesto—under the nominal influence of Eliot, A. N. Whitehead, Jacques Maritain, and the new psychologism—calling for a poetry which rejects "that acedia and unabashed glorification of the subjective so prominent in the world since the Reformation," yet proclaiming their faith in the order of tradition: "All genuine poetry is in a sense the formation of private spheres out of a public chaos: and therefore we would remind those who annually criticize us [the younger poets] for a lack of homogeneity, first, that on the whole it is environment which conditions values, not values which form environment."[1] Shifting the blame from self to environment, from spirit to matter, the poets lamented the helplessness of the common mind to escape the "acedia" which resulted from the "glorification of the subjective"; they could offer only a tentative hope that the poet might once again be the agent through whom the subjective self and his culture could be reconciled. This conflict of generations, they recognized, was perennial and universal; but present history had brought it to a most violent head. The crisis was religious, cultural, ethical, and psychological—a crisis thrust upon the poet that had once been the problem of the church and of other traditional institutions. The age demanded a new engagement of poetry, denying the kind of universal resolution to the universal crisis Eliot had discovered in the Fisher King myth, in the usable past, or in the church militant. Ironically, this deference to the primacy of environment would be easily transferable from an Eliotic stress on the a priori of tradition to a Marxist-oriented idealism.

This is a vague enough manifesto, strategically and humorously blurred; and after the fact it can be seen merely to apologize for the kind of stylistic experiments Auden and Day Lewis contributed to the volume. Implicitly, however, the declaration analyzes the softness of Day Lewis' earlier two volumes, which were so blatantly public in style yet sentimentally private—poems, that is, formed almost entirely from and by the values and the language of a dying culture's dying art. The poet's first order of business, the editors recognized, lay in the realm of language which, caught between the counterclaims of the Classic and Romantic (or between I. A. Richards' dichotomies, denotation and connotation), reflected the ultimate dualisms that lay at the heart of present crises. The new poetry, seeking not so much radically new values as enduring ones, must, in Eliot's sense, reassociate the sensibility—not by denying the present but by discovering its language in the present, in the "environment which conditions values." The Metaphysical poets might serve as guide, as they did for Eliot, but in no sense could the poet comfort himself that he shared in a timeless order of literary monuments or in a metaphysical great chain. The poet stood at the frontier, but he was also heir to a failed tradition to which he was emotionally tied. His task was to find in the present that which might link past and future, to find the language, as it were, which would not only allow communication between the two but ease the transition between them. As Day Lewis would insist in *Transitional Poem,* the one mode of unity remaining in the modern world was the unity of mind—

Whitehead's dream that, by understanding the "emergent evolution" of mind, we might discover the continuity between man and his environment. A measure of that continuity was embedded in language. And what the language of a technological age manifested, Day Lewis later argued in *A Hope for Poetry,* was that intellect has outrun emotions, forcing modern man to live a life of divided allegiance to past and present (42).

II   *College Pastoral*

Day Lewis went up to Wadham College, Oxford, in 1923. Two years later he published, at his own expense, *Beechen Vigil, and Other Poems,* a small collection of twenty-four poems. More than two years after this publication another twenty-four appeared in *Country Comets.* The two collections may only be called, even in the most generous sense, juvenilia. There is little evidence of development from one to the other; yet *Transitional Poem,* which was certainly in progress when these collections appeared, seems scarcely related to them in either theme or style. In *The Buried Day,* Day Lewis describes the pride with which he assaulted Oxford as a fledgling poet and the diffidence with which he continued to write poems even after the frigid reception of *Beechen Vigil* in London (168). *Country Comets* obviously marks the culmination of the undergraduate years, just as *Transitional Poem* is his declaration, not to say enactment, of rebirth. They are both, interestingly enough, essentially love poems—the one, an idyl of youthful desire; the other, a mature confrontation of the meaning and structure of love.

Day Lewis was twenty-one when *Beechen Vigil* appeared, a testimony to the isolation of a dream-spent youth. A painfully naïve grouping of verse of Victorian and Georgian vintage, the poetry is Rupert Brooke at play. There is little originality in the volume, not even any imaginative initiative or remarkable energy. Yet they are poems seriously devoted to themselves—more than anything else, they are evidence of a commitment to vocation. The first, entitled "The Net," reads:

> Poet, sink the shining net
>   In ebb and flow
> Only there thy spoil is met
>   Where all tides go.
>
> Bend above the wavering net.

> These silvery hordes
> Often shall o'releap the cords,
> And thou shalt fret
>
> For so much beauty unharvested.
> Some hour shall bless,
> And thou one lasting gleam shall add
> To loveliness.   (7)

Discouragingly, this poem is one of the volume's best—a poem true only to the opacities of a young poet's vision and to his own consuming self-importance. The book, on the whole, is an anthology of idle dreams, a paean to innocence and ethereal pleasures, filled with the misty emotions of childhood years, of idyllic love, and of the poet's privileged intercourse with permanence. "The Net" does not caution one to gather rosebuds but indulges the cliché that the poet must grasp absolutes, or perhaps gleams of eternity, in the "net" of lyric form. One of the more palatable poems, "Late Summer" (23), explores the pastoral clichés of vanished years, the years since Day Lewis' childhood at bucolic Edwinstowe; and this theme possesses him again and again in later years, not always fortunately. But "Late Summer" is not so much from the memory of a boy's youth as from his reading of Georgian anthologies. It joins with other laments for the lost Arcady of youth ("Lost"[20]; "Once in Arcady" [25]; "Sanctuary" [28]) to confirm the volume's tone and to give authority to the youthful poet who again and again has cast his net after fleeting loveliness.

Perhaps the most revealing single poem, however, is "Rose-Pruner," which was to become the joke of his Oxford years. "Rose-Pruner" (11) imitates the Georgian affinity for the colloquial, speaking through the voice of "Old Tom the pruner" who, being short-sighted, prunes off a "young shott"; and, when told of it, he suggests that even God may be getting old and myopic since he pruned off Tom's "son," the "young green o' the tree" prematurely. If the idiom is supposed to suggest Day Lewis' Irish heritage, it is stage Irish, just as the Hardyesque fatalism is a schoolboy mood and not at all convincing. The poem has something of that quality which has made Wordsworth's poems of the good, innocent man laughable, but it has none of Wordsworth's redeeming qualities, especially his sense of a grace-filled nature.

But "Rose-Pruner" does anticipate the mood of *Country Comets,* which is preeminently the volume of youth's discovering time. This second book is dedicated to Day Lewis' bride-to-be: "To her whose mind and body are a poetry I have not achieved I give these poems."

But the object of his devotion is in reality disembodied, the young poet's unachievable ideal; and the mood of the book hangs upon the nostalgia of loss: of the poet's vision, of his language—in effect, of emotion. Love is linked with transience; nature is explored as a projection of post-adolescent desire; and the poet, having lost youth's magical world view, lives as an alien in nature with only the faintest memory of his clouds of glory.

Though one poem, "Cyprian! Cyprian" (5), assumes an antirational pose and, in the word if not the spirit of Lawrence, proclaims a poetry of the "body," the dominant theme is sentimental loss. In the Keatsian "Naked Women of Kotyle" (7), the maker falls in hopeless love with his creation, the woman-in-the-verse. In "Retrospect: From a Street in Chelsea" (17), "The Only Pretty Ring-Time" (18), and "My Love Came to Me" (25), the subject is lost love—"They are all gone into the past." Andrew Marvell, indeed, and Keats are the volume's forefathers; but their poetry is filtered through the limp decorums of Georgian style. "Glutton Time, be not so greedy/ For my slim and subtle lady" (32) is the theme one poem advances, with only the faintest anticipation of the Anglo-Saxon alliteration Day Lewis later adoped from Gerard Manley Hopkins and Wilfred Owen. But it does show a firm command of Georgian sentimentalism. In sum, the book is dedicated to the "purple" sentiments of failure: "Now stands the poet with his bottle/ Of cut glass by the waterfall,/ To trap the rainbows glittering there;/ Gloating he comes to his dark study—/ O, the rainbow he would enthrall/ Is a few waterdops, its rare/ Essence eludes him . . ." (3). Strangely enough, the sentiments and even the metaphors recall Ralph Waldo Emerson's "Each and All," but there is no hint of a sustaining transcendental vision—or of any sustaining mode of thought whatsoever.

Setting poetry against science and reason, identifying it with dream, Day Lewis exploited the conventions which placed the enduring reality of poetry against the ephemeral reality of the world. The landscape of his idyl is that of memory or nostalgia; his nature, the environment of childhood innocence; his lady, an idealized loved possessed only in romantic anticipation. It is pastoral and pagan, a remote world of his childhood superimposed upon one derived from books. For the experience of these two volumes is almost exclusively drawn from the library: the summers of youth mythicized and held timeless in his memory. But his memory is poetic, self-deceptive, artificial; his paganism, only a stance.

III *Well Out of Eden*

It is little wonder that *Transitional Poem* confronts experience as a secular analogy of the Fall, at once painful and fortunate, regretful yet desired. Several years later, Day Lewis was to remark in *Buried Day* about this contradictory pull of his nostalgia: "I experience when I move house a delightful illusion of better things to come, of being reborn. But this sanguine, forward-looking self is counterweighted by a self both nostalgic and melancholy, a self which hates leaving places" (89). If this statement reveals the psychological dualism of transition, it no less manifests something of the tensions which stimulate the vital life of the mind. This desire to live in new houses that pulls against the securities of the space once comfortably occupied (the house of childhood, orderly and complete) is no doubt a metaphor of poetic tension. The desire to compose a new space demands the negation of previous space. Or as Gaston Bachelard has explained, the poet is caught between the impulse to create a perfect poem and the awareness that such an ultimate creation would preclude the need of other poems and hence deny his continuing role as poet: "Maybe it is a good thing for us to keep a few dreams of a house that we shall live in later, always later, so much later, in fact, that we shall not have time to achieve it. For a house that was final, one that stood in symmetrical relation to the house we were born in, would lead to thought—serious, sad thoughts—and not to dreams. It is better to live in a state of impermanence than in one of finality."[2]

Though it is an error to consider *Transitional Poem* simply the product of this psychology, the dramatic conflict that gave force to Day Lewis' poetry in the 1930's can be traced to it. The personal tension finds its analogue in social and cultural necessity; the inbred pull of tradition is counterweighted by the urgency to escape a dying world and thus to lead the way to the frontiers of the new. On every level—personal, ethical, psychological, cultural—the conflict holds: hope counterbalanced by skepticism; anxiety, by anticipation.

Of *Transitional Poem*, Day Lewis was to observe many years later in *The Buried Day* that "the scars of [his] unique struggle with the philosophers are clearly visible" (185). While it is true enough that the poem stems directly from a bout with philosophical abstractions, the struggle itself is the subject of the poem—a young man trying to bring his education into line with the confusion of his experience. For the poem presumes to record what Day Lewis had called the "prime development of this century, our experiment in the 'emergent evolution of mind.' " [3] It aspires to put a representative young self on record in such a way that that self will come to understand not simply its own unique nature but also the nature of the mature social self into which it is evolving. A poem of growing up, of the processes of growth, it begins by casting off the earlier self, but only by way of exploring what that self was and how it is integral to present consciousness.

Transitional Poem is a moderately long poem (1,142 lines) in four parts, consisting of thirty-four intellectual lyrics of various forms. Rather than assuming a style, it is in search of a style—the style of the emerging and developing mind. Still, it has its structural order and its dialectical integrity. The epigraphs to the four parts suggest that thematic concern. The first is from Maximian (and from Day Lewis' Latin training), stressing a faith in the enduring unity of mind; the last, from Auden, stresses the advent of a new age which will put that faith to a severe test. The middle two are from Walt Whitman and Herman Melville, respectively, authors who verify the centrality of the creative self in the world that had lost all other centers. But the essential style of the poem is provided by Eliot: a pastiche of imitations and echoes, it includes notes in the first edition. This style is that of an individual talent emerging from a received tradition of styles which comprise its formal and informal education: in Day Lewis' case, from the Latin through the Metaphysicals up to Yeats and Eliot and beyond to the frontiers with Auden. The allusion to two classical figures of American literature, at a time when the American consciousness had a limited appeal in the English universities, suggests a great deal about Day Lewis' radical leap beyond his Georgian orientation and something about the abandoned self of the poet without a viable past. This remarkable (and self-conscious) assimilation of influences results in a formidably intellectual, but often painfully naïve and obscure, poem.

Day Lewis has said that the four parts operate respectively on four integral levels of meaning: Part One, the metaphysical, the self isolated in modern chaos with only the immanent order of mind—"the tetragonal/ Pure symmetry of brain"—as its identity; Part Two, the ethical, or the essential unity (and interinvolvement) of minds that alone may redeem the isolated self from moral chaos; Part Three, the psychological conflict of the divided self that results from the fall into self-consciousness; and Part Four, the esthetic which alone can synthesize the other three on the level of immediate experience, redeeming the fall by bringing the self out of isolation and into the realm of shared experience with other selves. In effect, the poem is an exercise in confronting the modern problem outlined by Auden and

Day Lewis in their Preface to *Oxford Poetry, 1927:* the metaphysical, ethical, and psychological chaos of the modern mind must be confronted first by the creative (imaginatively synthesizing) man. Language is at the center of the problem, for man is language. And the crisis of the modern self is manifest in the chaos of language, the incoherence of modern thought. *Transitional Poem* is an apology for the poet, for the creative self which, in its transition from youth to manhood, discovers the true significance and responsibility of its vocation. To possess the future is to create its language.

The first two poems of Part One state directly the modern self's dilemma. Given the dramatic alienation of man from nature and hence the disintegration of the Romantic vision, the poet must assume the primacy of mind over nature, or rather the primacy of mind *within* nature:

> It is certain we shall attain
> No life till we stamp on all
> Life the tetragonal
> Pure symmetry of brain. (*Collected Poems,* 13)

"But there is naught surprising/ Can explode the single mind" (14). The notes Day Lewis added to the poem (whether in imitation or in mockery of Eliot is hard to determine) suggest Spinoza as the source of this faith; but, for Day Lewis, it is a Spinoza called to answer for the failures of Romanticism and religion, for man cast out of an orderly universe into one where the only appeal is to his own mind. Rejecting nothing, committed to facing "All elements or none," scorning appeals to God, or deductions from cosmic order, the poem begins by sweeping away every truth but the immanent order of mind. In fact, Whitehead, not Spinoza, would appear in the "emergent evolution of mind " to be the immediate patron of the poet's faith; for the organicism of Whitehead's process theory had salvaged something of the Romanticism which Day Lewis generation had lost and which it so desperately sought in its strategies of impersonal creation.

This is no easy commitment; for, as the third poem states, the temptation is always to take the easy way, to fall back upon the old fatalism, or to embrace the old certitudes. The situation of this poem, in fact, is the isolation of two lovers; the style is indirect and enigmatic and, like the poet's mind, wavering but not submissive. Assuming he is "lord of/ Something," the poet then resists the easy way: seeking the "instant realized" for what it is, taking the way of love, and lying down today "with finite" so that tomorrow he may lie "with infinite." His love is the "potency of earth," passionate and untamed; but his embrace of her is the necessary beginning.

In this sense, *Transitional Poem* is a love poem that exploits the young man's awakening to himself and to his physical desire for the other as a metaphor of the metaphysical quest for order. Turning from idealized past to fallen present, from "fossil certitudes" to a world in which only the order of mind can be assumed, the fledgling self must embrace the earth before it can pursue the ideal. "Our Mean" replaces "Omnipotence" as the center (15). And the resolution to metaphysical despair—that radical dualism which separates self from nature and brings into question cosmic order—is imaged in the sexual union of poet and loved one:

> My love is a tower.
> Standing up in her
> I parley with planets
> And the casual wind. (17)

This slyly erotic metaphor is extended toward the metaphysical. And Part One moves toward conclusion by equating the unity of two lovers with the only possible access man has to cosmic certitude (fifth and sixth poems). The fall into self-consciousness presents the poet with a world of "antinomies"; he cannot reinvoke the child's vision of oneness with nature, cannot "grip those skirts of cloud [which] the matriarch sky" reaches down to him, though that is the unity he desires. For the mind's "forked speculations" (again, the sexual metaphor for a philosophical condition), only love is available, the love which leads the mind back to intercourse with earth and to its first task of imposing order there.

Part One concludes, then, with the poet's assuming his vocation. Whatever order he stamps upon his world will be one of words; yet it will not be "abstract art" but a direct embrace of the world, a new relation. The significant discovery at the end of Part One, in fact, is that the poet's vocation rests in constant search for order, which, like the woman in the act of love, is never finally possessed:

> Phrase-making, dress-making—
> Distinction's hard to find;
> For thought must play the mannequin, strut in phrase,
> Or gape with the ruck: and mind,
> Like body, from covering gets
> Most adequate display. (19)

The incurable dualism makes all reality transient. Thoughts, like the body, are dressed in the style of their moment and have their existence in that style; yet thoughts, unlike the body, are universal or ideal, and may survive self. This faith in the reality of mind in itself certifies the essential rule of the poet as maker, as shaper of order in a world devoid of any other center. For the incessantly made new world repudiates "fossil certitudes," by re-dressing them in the texture of immediate feeling. But this new language of love fixes the center in the interpersonal relation of love. It eyes "God askance," denying Him as center and with Him the old world view.

The obscurities of *Transitional Poem* are the result essentially of Day Lewis' overwhelming ambition for his poem. He wants to write out of the experience of the moment: the shock of his university education which had led to a progressive rejection of the immediate past; the discovery of love's rejuvenating power; the philosophical confusions of the present day muddled in the young poet's mind with his own spiritual bewilderment. But he finds in the moment a theme of high seriousness and a style almost equal at times to its metaphysical gravity. The constant shift between personal and intellectual reference, the borrowings from Spinoza, the echoes of John Donne, the aggressive tone—all are the products of a poem and of a poet in search of a style and an enduring language, of a tradition uncluttered by the excrescences of the Romantic. The poem is, of course, an intensely personal, romantic one.

Part Two, which begins with the epigraph from Whitman, rejects old allegiances for new. In an echo of both Whitman and Yeats, Day Lewis announces that it is time to stand up and declare for those he has "loved and chosen." Just as he did in Part One, he again casts off his "schoolboy clout" and his allegiance to tradition in order to "learn the grammar of my days"; and he nominates as tutors the few who have nourished him in his transition: the first, "who ground my lust to love," is Mary King, his wife; the second, Rex Warner, an intellectual guide (in a much later poem, Day Lewis commemorated his lifelong friendship with Warner by quoting the lines about the "hawk-faced man" [*The Gate*]); the third, a remarkable woman named Margaret Marshall who at a fortunate time during his college years guided him through a period of postadolescent intellectual confusion; and lastly Auden, "Conduct's Old Dobbin, thought's chameleon," whose "all too stable universe" evinced the triumph of the "single mind" over the "split intelligence" (21). These mentors have shown him the possibilities, if not the actuality, of a new vision; but the responsibility for achieving it returns upon the individual self. The remaining nine poems of Part Two explore the consequences of his commitment.

In effect, these poems pare cosmic vision down to human community. That is, embracing a world in which the human is no longer deducible from the divine, in which myth and belief are destroyed, the poet can aspire only to a radically attenuated vision. Part Two, devoted to the ethical, is a manifest example of what Day Lewis later called his "romantic humanism." The ninth renounces despair, the idiocy of brooding over time; yet in the tenth one he reminds himself that, with the disappearance of the heroic and of the transcendent frontiers to be crossed, the self is challenged by "recent/ Ambition," which is the source of the "ancestral curse," Adam's self-knowledge. In short, Day Lewis tries to catch in these lyrics the tensions of his new life—the pull, in one way, of the ideal; in the other, of the drably real; the desire for the heroic and the knowledge that, in forfeiting the "fossil certitudes," he has denied the heroic. For, with the disappearance of the old sustaining beliefs, the ethical absolute is vanquished; and man, as in the twelfth poem, is left with desire (his sexual appetite) but without the myths which will contain and formalize it. He is caught in the humanist dilemma: he desires the ethical absolute but is condemned to the relatives of time. Heart and head must both be honored. The anxiety of sex, in fact, is that its vital necessity may urge him toward the absolutely irrational where, as with Lawrence, he re-creates Paradise or unity as the opposite of consciousness. This paradox is the crux of the poem's dialectic. For Day Lewis, any denial of time and space, of the dualistic present, in order to seek an all-embracing unity, is another manifestation of the self's death wish: "I see the constellations,/ But by their gaps."[4] Reason gives him identity, but diminishes his stature.

The fourteenth poem, a crucial lyric of Part Two, begins:

> In heaven, I suppose, lie down together
> Agonized Pilate and the boa-constrictor
> That swallows everything: but we must seize
> One horn or the other of our antitheses. (26)

This embrace of limitation (and hence of sex) rejects heaven where all is reconciled. The lyric is itself an interesting example of stylistic pastiche, with echoes of Milton and Eliot, Shakespeare and the Bible—the poet in the present set against, yet continuous with, his tradition. The poem collapses the personal crisis of the divided self with the historical dilemma, and for the first time in Day Lewis we can observe the relevance of politics and metaphysics in the ethical:

> Allow
> One jointure feasible to man, one state
> Squared with another—then he can integrate
> A million selves and where disorder ruled
> Straddle a chaos and beget a world. (26)

And so, like Noah, the poet sends out, from the "closet of the brain," a dove which returns to him with the promise of a new ground (27). This new ground begins in love—and, most vividly in poem fifteen, in the Mount Ararat of his love's breasts—for she is the world he has straddled. Love must be preserved against the exhaustible moments of desire and passion: against the paradox of sexual climax where fulfillment preludes a new division. Thus, Part Two concludes with a warning to the self not to lose itself in desire and to beware of the self-destructive impulse in the desire for unity, either physical or metaphysical:

> They say that a mathematician
> Once fell to such a passion
> For x and y, he locked
> His door to keep outside
> Whatever might distract
> Him from his heavenly bride:
> And presently died
> In the keenest of blisses
> With a dozen untasted dishes
> Outside his door. (29)

Drawing back from desire, from the lust for ultimate knowledge and from the poetry of apocalypse, Day Lewis commits himself both ethically and poetically to a middle ground. From there he will make his poetry work toward a new vision in the world, not for one beyond it:

> Let logic analyse the hive,
> Wisdom's content to have the honey;
> So I'll go bite the crust of things and thrive
> While hedgerows still are sunny. (31)

Part Three, which returns to the theme of the divided self, seeks psychological resolution. If the ethical perspective focused upon the poet's relation with other people, the psychological is preoccupied with the impact his new commitment has had upon the isolated self. Once more the conflict is between desire for the ideal and compromise with reality; and, analogously, between the subjective or intuitive self and the intellectual, rational self. In the eighteenth poem, perhaps the most remarkable in the entire series, the antinomies are imaged in the landscapes of Trojan and Greek worlds, the country and the city, hence emotion against intellect or unconscious set against conscious. Trojan passion is vital and violent, racked with desire whereas Greek reason is orderly and meditative but nearly devoid of life. The first is Dionysian; the second, Apollonian. The one, id; the other, ego. The poet is caught in a "rubbish heap" between "stream and city." His task is to reconcile the two by denying neither. On all levels—but primarily on the sexual one—the poet must come to terms with antinomies by creating his new time-space out of a vision which denies neither flesh nor spirit, passion nor intellect, love nor fear. If the fall into consciousness has been a painful birth, the mind retains the resources of its beginning, its primordial sense of an original unity. That primordial sense is what sustains him—the hope that makes poetry not only possible but urgently necessary—for the moment of the creative act is the one in which the self renews itself by experiencing its own primal identity.

At nearly every climax in these lyrics a dominant motif emerges. Self-consciousness has left the self floundering, like Donne's "sublunary lovers," in a dullness which human love cannot perfectly repair; yet, it is human and not divine love, the natural not the ideal, out of which any future world must be made:

> There's no star in the sky
> But gazing on it makes it double
> And the infatuate eye
> Can breed dilemmas in it.
>
> Wiser it were to sheath
> My burning heart in clay
> Than by this double breath
> To magnify the tomb. (36)

To sheath the heart in clay—to turn the passion of desire back upon the physical and away from the transcendental—is the poet's lone answer for the psychological schisms of desire. Love in the particular saves him from the self-consuming tendencies of love in general, turns him from some fruitless pursuit of the ideal or the consolations of traditional faith, as the twenty-third and twenty-fourth poems indicate:

> Farewell again to this adolescent moon;
>   I say it is a bottle
> For papless poets to feed their fancy on.
>   Once mine sucked there, and I dreamed

> The heart a record for the gramophone—
> One scratch upon the surface,
> And the best music of that sphere is gone. (38)

He must be reborn to the world in the act of sexual or profane love, in the "integrity that's laid bare/ Upon the edge of common furniture" (39).

Turning away from the ideal, rejecting the possibility of ultimate knowledge, and denying the "central stone," the poet solves psychological alienation by projecting himself into the brute and common ground:

> For individual truth must lie
> Within diversity;
> Under the skin all creatures are one race,
> Proved integers but by their face.
>
> So he, who learns to comprehend
> The form of things, will find
> They in his eye that purest star have sown
> And changed his mind to singular stone. (40)

The psychological problem, then, must be confronted as were the metaphysical and ethical. Truth lies in the intercourse of antinomies: in the power of the sexual act, in the overriding rhythms of "fear and love," in the life principle of repulsion and attraction as Day Lewis glosses the phrase in a note.[5] (The awkward and forced syntactical inversion of the next-to-last line quoted above is evidence of the intrusive power of *idea* in this poem and of the sacrifices of lyric grace that Day Lewis had to make in his transition.) The poet's urge is toward an equilibrium of those forces, on every level, an equilibrium premised on "passionate cleavage." Thus "love and fear," like the essential opposites of life and death, lie at the center of mind, reconcilable only in the thematic alternations within the poem, which veritably imitate the rhythms of the sexual act. For the act of sexual love not only gives life but wears out life; it is integral to death (41–42). Assuming his intellectual majority, he is left to confront these perdurable opposites without the consoling myths or the traditional forms of faith. Yet there is implied here, in this field of necessary antinomies, the ground of Day Lewis' later communism—the essential community of mind, of selves, reflected in the intercourse of opposites: "Under the skin all creatures are one race."

Part Four attempts to contain the earlier three perspectives within the esthetic. "*In the beginning*," the twenty-eighth poem opens: "*was the Word.*" And the poet weaves the biblical motif of the Incarnation into a modern secular form: " 'the word,' in this poem," Day Lewis has remarked, "stands for the individual poetic impulse, as a part of the Logos in the theologian's sense of mind expressing God in the world."[6] The poet has fallen into the world—"you are well out of Eden"—but in and through him alone is the Word or the higher order to be made manifest. A new world is a new language and thus a new center or logos. And the poet reaches to embrace his fallen world: "for there's no wonder where all things are new;/ No dream where all is sleep; no vision where/ Seer and seen are one"; and he will not, like Poe, lament his loss of Israfel's realm. Life is where opposites generate it—in conflict—and poets must give flesh to the Word only in the world which lacks the Word. Life, in fact, is fleshed out in the opposites of chaos and cosmos, of flux and motion moving toward form. The poem, and the making of poems, not only imitates but creates reality. This creation of the single mind is the order aspired to by man.

Hence the poet turns his back on the world of innocence he is leaving—the chaos of passions and desires never understood—and sets about the task of directing those energies upon the fallen world (46—47). And in the last three poems he reassesses his own strong desire and the difficulty of understanding or directing his passion. That, indeed, is the crisis of transition, to find his own roots: a place from which those energies might be released creatively rather than destructively. The thirty-third poem is a nearly private lyric about the poet's taking up his first home—it offers an image of achieved order and of the advent of the mature self: "This is the interregnum of my year;/ All spring except the leaf is here,/ All winter but the cold" (49). And the final poem, using the extended metaphor of the hawk hovering at a distance above the earth, which allows him a prospect of its "black contours," provides an image of esthetic perspective. First experience, then contemplation; first descent, then ascent—but there is always a perspective that maintains the antinomies of self and earth, mind and object, never the ultimate perspective of omnipotence.

Transitional Poem closes on this note. The poet, having entered time fully, comes to engage the flux with mind, to bring the word by which alone the "tetragonal/ Pure symmetry of brain" (man's metaphysical, ethical, psychological, and esthetic knowledge of himself and his world) can be stamped upon life without denying its throbbing pulse.[7] The four parts lead to the same conclusion and, for Day Lewis as poet, to the beginning. Indeed, *Transitional Poem* brings Day Lewis to the threshold of poetry, and hence to engagement.

In this poem he affirmed the style of his time: cerebral and detached and allusive, metaphorical, self-consciously attentive to maintaining its multi-leveled meanings discrete one from the other. But most obvious is the conscientiousness with which Day Lewis tries to avoid subjective poetry, to turn the private experience inside out by way of indicating its communal relevance. What he sought in this style was a perspective upon his personal experience from which he might analyze it in terms of universals; but the analysis was not be be—as he said in the Preface to *Oxford Poetry, 1927*—the analysis of emotion "recollected in tranquillity." On the contrary, the emotional and the intellectual, the synthesis and analysis, must be one: the poem must catch the moment when experience becomes real by coming into the analytical and comprehensive realm of consciousness; but it must do so before it has become past experience, drained of its immediacy by recollection. All of which is an argument for an immediate intellectual style and for a poetry of ideas that is also a poetry of action—a poetry of realized subjectivity. The "emergent evolution of mind" is the emergence of a new language out of an old.

The most important thing *Transitional Poem* anticipates about the decade of English poetry to follow its publication is the recognition that poetry must in some way be made a social and moral instrument again—not to serve an establishment, nor even to analyze the deficiencies of the past—but as a mode leading toward a new synthesis of values. It suggests why, before the political pressures became overt, Day Lewis, along with Auden, discovered the urgency of a new, committed poetry. Although the influence of I. A. Richards on the pedagogical tenor of this mode is not to be disregarded, this poetry is, most of all, the survival of a traditional religious and moralistic instinct that speaks with such force. The political dimensions of Day Lewis' later poetry are implicit in this earlier poem. The recurrent motif of the single mind realizing its full potential within an encompassing order is residually political. Transition, the journey toward some mysterious frontier and vague new world of consciousness, did not necessarily presume a radical dismissal of the past; on the contrary, the transition was to be gradual and continuous with the past, incorporating whatever of tradition was enduring. Above all, it was a search for the community of minds that spares the isolated mind. The sifting of tradition for the buried self was the poet's chief role. But he had to bring this self into the present, into consciousness, and hence into conflict with itself. This necessary risk of "love and fear" made continuity possible. Through the risk of turning away from "fossil certitudes" and toward the uncertain future, the Word might again be restored to the world; for the Word is the disclosure, through language, of the mystery of origins and the primordial urge of life from chaos to order.

CHAPTER 3

The Poetics of Action

IN the four years following *Transitional Poem,* Day Lewis' poetic energies were directed at two equally long poems, *From Feathers to Iron* (1931) and *The Magnetic Mountain* (1933). Each confirms the style and, in effect, the commitments of the earlier piece. And in each, Day Lewis comes more directly under the influence of Auden and his literary interests—more self-consciously derivative in the struggle to find an individual style. *From Feathers to Iron* begins where *Transitional Poem* leaves off: the self who assumes this maturity and its responsibilities in the earlier poem must now acknowledge his own creative obligations; he must recognize change (history) and the price that commitment to it exacts. *The Magnetic Mountain,* on the other hand, is a more overtly engaged poem, and more explicitly directed at the social dimensions of the earlier commitment and, to its detriment, one more polemical and propagandistic than anything which precedes it.

There is, therefore, a progressive concentration and constriction throughout the three poems. The political implications which were residual in *Transitional Poem* emerge to dominate the *The Magnetic Mountain.* But they are only occasionally explicit in the allegorical overlay of *From Feathers to Iron.* One explanation of this thematic narrowing from intellectual analysis to the polemics of action lies in the rapidly changing history of the times; another, in Day Lewis' own insistence that poetry must be made to affect history and that the poet alone could be the responsible agent of values in transition. It would take Day Lewis but a few short years to learn the full significance of Auden's line, "poetry makes nothing happen." But the early 1930's, as Day Lewis came to acknowledge, was an "absurdly credulous" period, introducing an unsettled decade which inspired intellectual hopes unavailable to and unbelievable by any time since.

By the end of *Transitional Poem,* Day Lewis was convinced that the poetic analysis of self—the poem which caught the mind in the moment of its emergent evolution—was to be the primary mode of his day: that one could begin with the self as object and extend that self-knowledge to the universal. Hence the four levels of *Transitional Poem* presumed at the same time to analyze personal experience in universal categories and to catch the simultaneity of the categories as they function in conscious experience. The synthesis of the metaphysical, the ethical, and the psychological in the esthetic was, in effect, an attempt to establish the poet in a divisive age as the sole being capable of reuniting act and idea in experience. But, if at the end of *Transitional Poem* the poet "come(s) into my peace" (50), the peace was achieved at the threshold of history. Thrown into time, the poet would have to confront history's processes directly, and the oneness of act and idea would not be so easily realized. The ambitious allegorical structure of *From Feathers to Iron* is an attempt to maintain the simultaneity of the idea in the act—to dramatize the complex moral, metaphysical, and psychological involvement of man in his intimate relations with others and with the future community all are obligated to create. *The Magnetic Mountain,* which dispenses with the dialectical structure of the earlier poems, uses the idea as a call to action. It heralds an action, however, that, in a most ironic sense, can only be realized beyond the poem; the poem calls, that is, for a "change of heart" and exhorts us to a moral journey. The realization of the idea is to follow the act; the anticipation of the idea is to motivate and sustain the act. But the lyrical voice and even the intellectual vitality of the earlier poems are radically throttled in the process.

I *The Journey*

The structural organization of Day Lewis' poetry in the early 1930's rests almost exclusively on the metaphor of the journey. Obviously, the journey has its roots in a literary and mythic tradition, and its meanings in the poetry of the decade is renderable in archetypal and religious terms. It is similarly obvious that both Day Lewis and Auden are as conscious as they are unconscious of the journey's symbolic import. This self-critical, as well as intuitive manipulation of the quest myth, is what, in fact, saves Auden's poetry at crucial points from spilling over into a narrow political or moral allegory, just as it enables Day Lewis to extend the political arguments of his poetry beyond the parochial limitations of politics and ideology. Auden, feeling the depth, resonance, and psychological immediacy of the myth, saw that it lay at the origin of man's need for order and hence preceded politics or ideology. He saw, that is, that the experience of the quest—the psychic dislocation, the alien landscape that lies between the home or womb man has left, and the end of the journey, the psychologically sublime future itself—were the universals which explained not only social conservatism but the emotional violence of personal commitment. In this sense primarily, politics could be married with poetry as an integrally humanist theme.

Auden's young man camping out on the frontier—significantly, in a poem first called "Ode to My Pupils" and later "Which Side Am I Supposed to Be On?"—dramatizes the divided self of the poet in the 1930's. On the one hand, the poet has made his intellectual commitment and is now the teacher; on the other, he remains identified with his pupils and thus with his earlier self, suffering the very anxieties of the transition for which he consciously opts. Or, in other words, he is divided between his idealistic commitment to the future and his emotional ties with the past, between his desire to sacrifice the self and his deep-seated conservative instincts toward preservation of the status quo ante. That Auden saw the developing ideological conflicts first in terms of a psychodrama, and the psychodrama as a manifestation of archetypal tensions, suggests the enduring depth of his poetry which survives the occasions of *Realpolitik*. Day Lewis, working out of the discoveries of *Transitional Poem*, was ready to acknowledge the same priority of experience to ideology. But the gradually increasing pressures of the decade had the ultimate effect upon him of forcing the political into prominence and of destroying the propitious balance that keeps poetry in the realm of immediate experience.

The divided self is Day Lewis' theme from beginning to end—hence the essential journey. If *Transitional Poem* brought the self into its intellectual majority, confirming the primacy of mind (collective mind) in the evolution of cultural order, it divorced the self from its ancient and timeless home—from the ideal of community only faintly hinted at in the disintegrating memories of childhood security and in his nostalgia for tradition. Transition, indeed, implies not so much a willful departure from some ideal past as the deliberate assumption of the responsibility for seeking the ideal future, after being expelled from that past. In other words, the journey motif seeks its end in its beginning; it is a return to the ideal community, one occasionally conceived as the ideal or Communist state, but symbolically as the ideal reconciliation of the individual self with the estranged other. The journey, then, is through selfhood to selflessness—hence its anxieties and the recurring motif of creative self-sacrifice. Love is the poet's aspiration, the ideal of reconciliation and renewal. And love is community, somewhere beyond desire.

The journey in both Auden and Day Lewis has two stages: (1) expulsion from the old order, from falling Eden and from suffocating womb; (2) the precarious, existential search through an alien and threatening landscape toward some vaguely sensed new order, a rebirth of the isolated self into some new community. The second and most significant stage of the journey is always away from the ugly familiar toward the mysterious, evanescent ideal: from complexity and conflict to simplicity and order, from city to country, from fear to faith. But the journey is never complete; its life is in its psychic, moral immediacy. Auden's early psychological landscapes, inhuman and threatening yet pure and uncorrupted, offer vivid examples of the terrain of initiation where the self is purified of will and experiences a "change of heart." They are not prophetic, but here and now.

As the titles suggest, Edward Upward's *Journey to the Border* (1938) and Rex Warner's *The Wild Goose Chase* (1937) offer interesting fictional variations on what is perhaps the dominant emblematic figure of the decade. Warner's novel sets forth in striking detail this allegorical motif in which the "Auden Group" came to focus intensely the critical, moral, and ethical issues of its day. Using the grail quest as the controlling myth, Warner superimposes it with deliberate allegorical firmness upon his abstraction of the modern technological state. The "long journey beyond the froniter,"[1] which is the annual vegetation cum political rite of the state, is a mysterious imperative which is thrust upon its initiates by a community which no longer really understands the journey's purpose. The community, having lost its instinctual mythical understanding, has reduced its rituals to empty form or to the misty promise of personal material gain rather than self-sacrifice for the quester. The community's need for renewal has thus been reduced to competitive gamesmanship. But the urge for renewal asserts itself nevertheless in the form of the quest, a rite which all feel must be performed even if no longer understood. And the meaning of the quest is latently there in the minds of the quester: to "reclaim the land" (25), though the ideal end is no longer consciously believed in. The surviving instinct is the latent force of the old order and also a manifestation of the human will toward renewal. It is the human, subsuming generations and history.

What is important, however, is the mode of the present-day quest, whether authentic or artificial. Warner's three questers, three brothers, set off in search of the wild goose by three different modes: Rudolph, the masculine representative of the militaristic, aristocratic, Fascist order, by motorbike (that is, by the mechanical force of modern technology); David, the effeminate intellectual, by a carefully equipped push-bicycle (that is, by the the discrete cultural or ideological guides of the past); and George, the simple, innocent young man who takes life as it is, by a rusty bicycle once the property of his father (that is, by his own inherent energies and an instinctive sense of the continuing decorums of tradition). Warner makes it emphatically obvious that George's is the proper mode. His motivations—looking neither forward to the ideal future nor backward to the ideal past, seeking only the rewards of a satisfied curiosity—are the necessary ones. The journey is not through actual space but into the time-space of the future self, across the psychic frontier where lies a new world (not unlike the old one and continuous with it) which is itself divided and at odds.

In this new world, the simple community of yeomen are subjected to the capitalist organization in the city which depends on the natural resources drained from the productive capacities of the country. Rudolph and David, who quickly pass through the country into the city, seek the various advantages of power that satisfy their personalities; they compromise with the power structure; and they are lost in its corrupt selfishness. George, too, while attracted by the country, is compelled finally to leave it for the city, but in time he is repelled by its derogation of communal responsibility and love. He then returns to the country to organize and lead a successful overthrow of the city, a victory made successful by clarity of mind, purity of purpose, and the commitment of love.

The political implications are obvious enough—but the psychological, ethical, and methaphysical overtones (what Auden termed the necessary "change of heart"), constitute the true index of what the journey meant to Day Lewis. Warner's novel features the political as a metaphysical-moral issue, but the overwhelming pressures of the topical force the novel toward polemics. Something of this pressure is responsible for Day Lewis' transformation of the journey motif, which has its roots in Eliot's use of the dying god and grail quest, into an instrument for social action. But his instinctual sense of the dangers politics held for poetry managed to save him from any total subordination of one to the other.

II   *The Creator's Burden*

It is revealing that *Transitional Poem* does not develop linearly but, like its concluding image of the hawk, circles in upon its theme. *From Feathers to Iron*, on the other hand, is deliberately and consciously linear, though the line leads back upon its own beginning. The difference is that the earlier poem is a philosophical exploration (analysis) of the fall into consciousness, into selfhood—of what it means to be "well out" of Eden. The fall did not occur *in* time, but *into* time—that is, the fall had no duration; and its meaning is not manifest in historical or dramatic event but in the moment of self-discovery. But, once in time, the self's acts are circumscribed by history, just as the self is sacrificed to it. Creative self-sacrifice, indeed, it the preeminent theme of *From Feathers to Iron,* and the obvious fact that the time of the poem parallels Day Lewis' reactions during the incubation period of his first child should not detract from it. The process, moving from conception to birth, parallels the poet's own journey from one world to another, his own "change of heart," the restorative power of love to bring the self out of the isolated ego into community. Celebrating birth, the poem sings ironically the creator's (the male's) role as planter of the seed which he can only helplessly observe develop in the world-womb (female), ultimately to replace him, the father.

From Feathers to Iron, like *Transitional Poem*, is full of literary echoes: Donne, Eliot, Wordsworth, Yeats. The title is derived from Keats, the "three steps from feathers to iron" suggesting the stages of the self's growth from the securities of the womb (and dream) into the mechanical and material world of time (and thought). But the other epigraph, from Auden, is perhaps more revealing: "Do thoughts grow like feathers, the dead end of life?" Day Lewis must have known that the second phrase of Auden's line was taken almost verbatim from D. H. Lawrence's *Psychoanalysis and the Unconscious*. Thoughts are the excrescences of the mind and thus are the dead end of the vital process. Mind is the evolved product (epi-phenomenon) of matter. Hence only the vital process which ends in mind is alive, not the end product (idea) itself. And, ironically, the process of creation is equally the process of death. Thus we have the poem's governing paradox: the child's development in the womb, like the growth of seedling thoughts in the poet's mind, is the mark of his own process toward death. The hope the poet draws from this realization is the old one—the renewal of birth. The finite self is sacrificed to the greater vital process rather than being the culmination of it. He will be renewed in the new community of the family and, ultimately, live on in his creation.

This paradox may explain the poem's conscious manipulation of the wasteland and grail-quest motifs. In this instance, however, as contrasted with Eliot's poem, the quest leads to rebirth and rejuvenation: the poet begets upon his world, as within his wife, that which renews both, though it exacts a part of their independent selves, feeding upon them for its life. Born into time, the self must assume the responsibility of reproducing and extending its kind; and this responsibility is communal, not personal. The structure of the poem is overtly and consciously archetypal: moving from autumn to spring, from time through the nascence of death of the self to rebirth, it bridges time's divisive flux; and it celebrates the self's (and mind's) role in the natural and necessary process of birth-death-renewal. In analogy with the process of the child's birth, the mind must seek in the iron world of the present—in the technological landscape of the modern world—those evidences of organic process and vital renewal which nature once provided the Romantic imagination. Thus once again Day Lewis conducts his poem along multiple and discrete levels to the point where it often threatens to become patently allegorical.

Day Lewis, it appears, comes to depend so fully on the external time of the poem that he fails to give it a convincing internal order; its thematic unity, that is to say, rests almost entirely on his progressive reflection upon the fetus from its conception to its birth, with the overlay of mythic suggestion. The poem begins in the "dark" but sacred wood (of passion, the irrational) where love has its carnal moment, and it ends in the celebration of a new dawn (light, reason, order), proclaiming a "holiday" (a day both whole and holy) for the occasion. The birth proclaimed is a secular and civil parody of Christ's, and the new world He *incorporated*; the poet, a somewhat distressed Joseph musing upon what he, with miraculous help, has begot: the child, word, poem. Or, as Day Lewis has explained it for himself in *Buried Day*, "When . . . I was writing *From Feathers to Iron*, a sequence of poems whose subject matter was my personal experience during the nine months before the birth of my first child, I found that my own excitements and apprehension linked up quite spontaneously with a larger issue—the struggle and joy in which our new world should be born . . . " (218). The important fact, nonetheless, is that the political issues remain predominantly indirect; the larger issue of the new world is felt not in ideological but in intimate terms. The new world is an imperative in the wake of the fragmentation of the old, a pressure urgently felt on the level of the new family and manifest in the evolution of the poem itself.

The first five poems of the sequence are cautiously indirect and suggestive. They are poems of sexual intimacy, of the conception— reflecting both the speaker's faith in restorative sex and the mythical quester's anxiety over the nature and consequences of his role. Above all, they are poems of commitment:

> Nor fear we now to live who in the valley
> Of the shadow of life have found a causeway;
> For love restores the nerve and love is under
> Our feet resilient. Shall we be weary? (*Collected Poems*, 53).

The act of love is imaged in terms of vegetation rites: "There remains to/ Plough up the meadowland, reclaim the marshes" (54). This demands, in the second poem, a retreat from the town and in the third poem, "Back to the countryside." "You leave tonight for the Americas" (55), that figurative new world. The moment of departure is that of conception and its conferred responsibility. The key poem is the fourth one; out of the joy of the sexual climax is born all futures: joy, guilt, and all responsibilities. The journey launched in this moment is "no pleasure trip": "We carry freight/ To a certain end." The act of love is imaged in the collapsing of Freudian and technological terms, the train's thundering junction with the irrational, apocalyptic night. It is a beginning and an end. For in the fifth there is acknowledged the sacrifice of self attendant upon the creative act:

> We must a little part,
> And sprouting seed crack our cemented heart.
> Who would get an heir
> Initial loss must bear:
> A part of each will be elsewhere. (57)

The climax begets a physical and metaphysical synthesis and molds the unity of the future to which the individual self is sacrificed. The poet returns to the Renaissance paradox of *dying* and extends it into a dialectical myth of continuity The subsequent twenty-four lyrics survey the progenitor's emotions during the time of the child's (and the future world's) growth—a time of anticipation, joy, anxiety, fear, hope, and bewilderment. Creation breeds doubt; the new threatens the secure past; and the heightened life is anxiety. The maker loses control of his creation in his commitment to it. In terms of the poem's sexual metaphor, the father, having engendered his child, is left fretfully to contemplate the ambiguities of his act: he is isolated from the mother; he has begot upon her what may be her, and his own, destruction; he has fallen into a limbo (like the womb) between two worlds. He has relived the modern history of dualism and the paradox of origins. Thus the seventh poem, one of Day Lewis' more famous short pieces:

> Rest from loving and be living.
> Fallen is fallen past retrieving
> The unique flyer dawn's dove
> Arrowing down feathered with fire.
>
> Cease denying, begin knowing.
> Comes peace this way here comes renewing
> With dower of bird and bud knocks
> Loud on winter wall on death's door.
>
> Here's no meaning but of morning.
> Naught's soon of night but stars remaining,
> Sink lower, face, as dark womb
> Recedes creation will step clear. (58)

Celebrating the sacrifice and fulfillment of the fertility rite, the seventh poem links itself formally with the ancient poetry of the Anglo-Saxon tradition. The act of passion itself has quieted passion, and it has also thrust both husband and wife out of their isolated self-sufficiency and onto a mutual quest. The slow, deliberate, inexorable formation of the child in the womb signifies the organic inevitability of the new world and the vital principle (Day Lewis' Lawrencean heritage) on which the solidarity of that world is to be realized:

> Though we strike a new continent, it shall be
> Our islet; a new world, our colony.
> If we miss land, no matter. We've a stout boat
> Provisioned for some years: we need endure
> No further ill than to be still alone. (59)

The journey from conception to birth is no less from passion to reason (from id to ego, or instinct to order), the one essentially bound to the other. But the inevitable growth is attended by all the psychic dislocations that violent change effects. For the journey implies a commitment to time and, hence, consciously to death; or as the eleventh poem states, the transformations of the womb, where "negative's made positive," portend its opposite, the tomb where "positives change to negative." Life, like poetry, is a mirror that inverts images, uniting future with past, turning beginnings into ends.

The political dimensions of this poem are mainly latent, for the primal dislocations of the self in its act of passion and the moral readjustments of self to other (mate), looking toward a future community (the family), are featured in its predominant movements. Love resolves anxiety and desire by generating anxiety and desire. Hence, we have the recurrent motif: over the health of the fetus, the wife's suffering within the proximity of death, the uncertainty of the new world beyond the "frontier," which is to be the heritage of his son and not his own (64). The poet is suspended in anxiety but released by hope; and the alternation of moods creates a resonance by which alone the theme progresses. In other words, the themes constitute the act of creating the poem itself, for that is the ultimate implication of creative responsibility.

The twenty-first poem, which incorporates most of the tensions, opens with the poet-father addressing the unborn child, who is to repeat the rhythms of the poet's own life: his wasted and diverted energies, his thwarted desires, his aspirations and anticipations. The poem's allusiveness points specifically and ironically backward to *The Waste Land*: "Consider Phlebas, who shall be taller and handsomer than you" (69). If the son (or daughter) is to repeat the poet's history, however, if he is to suffer the division of self, he may learn that the rhythms of life (from unity to division, from womb to world to tomb) make alienation inevitable and point toward the possibility of a reclaimed future. Death is the one certainty, in other words, which exacts our commitment to making futures within the world and not beyond it, which compels us "to set house in order, bury/ The dead and count the living, consolidate,/ The soul against provided enemies" (69). Death is continuity. Hence, the escape from the wasteland is not through sacrificial action—but to an open and not a certain future:

> Planted out here some virtue still may flower,
> But our dead follies too—
> A shock of buried weeds to turn it sour.
> Draw up conditions—will the heir conform?
> Or thank us for the favour, who
> Inherits a bankrupt firm,
> Worn-out machinery, an exhausted farm? (70)

So at journey's end, as the birth approaches, the poet-father lives out his anxiety. As father, he has engendered the new hope and begotten pain, even perhaps death (73–74). But, more ominous still, he has begotten his own successor. The son is born into the sun; generation perpetuates generation. Thus the triumph of the vital principle of life over the isolated ego. The continuity of life depends on death which destroys the discontinuous self.

The Epilogue, in the form of a letter to W. H. Auden, coalesces the poem's themes. Composed in imitation of Auden's style, it celebrates his penchant for "nosing among/ Saxon skulls, roots of our genealogies" (76)—that is, Auden's exploration of the dark, internal landscape of the self in search of the vital roots and the traditional soil from which the individual has come and upon which his future community must be founded. In other words, this section affirms the essential traditionalism of the radical poets in the 1930's: the nostalgia and despair that divided their attentions and qualified their revolutionary commitments. Following Auden's lead, Day Lewis cautions his fellow poets to desert the soft, decaying south for the hard, cold, alien north—to follow the path from passion to reason, from the easy to the hard, from the flesh to the bone of reality. In other words, poets are to bring subjectivity to objectivity in language, just as the child brings id into ego, the self to intersubjectivity. The state, like the family, grows from the death of discontinuous selves. It grows from a personal to an interpersonal language.

Once again, as in *Transitional Poem*, the poem's end is a beginning. The fulfillment of one journey augurs another. The self made whole in its family is committed to time; the family microcosm anticipates the social macrocosm. The magic mountain always beckons and finding it lies only in the seeking. Thus Day Lewis' "romantic humanism" runs counter to the ideological absolute toward which it nevertheless forces him. The problem of his next poem, *The Magnetic Mountain*, is that it must prophesy and propagandize, exhorting the self toward a realized future and thus depart from the immediate experience which gave life to its predecessors. For while the earlier poems took as their theme the creation of a new language, *The Magnetic Mountain* sought to appropriate an ideology ready-made.

III   *The Necessary Future*

Stephen Spender, reflecting about his own divided loyalties in the 1930's, provides a convenient perspective from which to judge *From Feathers to Iron:*

In poetry I was confronted with the dilemma of stating a public emotion which had become a private one, and which yet became completely my own inner experience because ... it invaded my personality rather than sprang out of it. Critics like Virginia Woolf, who reproached our generation for writing too directly out of a sense of public duty, failed to see that public events had swamped our personal lives and usurped our personal experience. . . . I think I was probably right to enter deliberately into a confused situation, and reject the great simplifications of a deeply felt but impersonal public point of view. The truth of my existence was that . . . I did not plunge myself wholly in public affairs. Therefore a poetry which rejected private experience would have been untrue of me. Moreover, I dimly saw that the conflict between personal life and public causes must be carried forward into public life itself: it was my duty to express the complexity of an ambivalent situation. For our individualistic civilization to be born within the order of a new world, people must be complex as individuals, simple as social forces.[2]

Even in the 1950's, Spender's language retains the terminology of Romanticism which marked the attempt of these poets to synthesize the public and personal. In *From Feathers to Iron*, Day Lewis explores the mythical levels of the private for analogies with the public; the emergence into the public and communal, in fact, is the goal of the personal. In *The Magnetic Mountain*, on the other hand, we witness what Spender called the usurpation of the personal by the public—the willful coercion of the personal by the rational demands of the public. The public experience demands a social revolution, to which the personal, instinctual desire for rejuvenation must conform. The point of view is altered, therefore, by the shift from lived experience to ideological (or at least social) conviction.

Strangely enough, and perhaps unfortunately for the poem, *The Magnetic Mountain* does not dramatize that journey to and beyond the frontier, which it seems to promise. Revealingly, the poem's stress is on the sublime structure of the mountain rather than on the inner compulsion of the quester. There is no longer time to indulge the private sphere, no longer any significance in his personal anxiety or in the harrowing fear attendant upon uprootedness. The poem begins with its commitments fully made; its strategy is to defend and amplify those commitments: the ideal of the mountain which exists not in history but in men's desire for order and peace.

In this sense, the magnetic mountain is the symbol of the human spirit: it is an ideal beyond time and space, the gravitational center of man's need for community from which history has alienated him. Its origin lies in Romantic aspiration, but it offers to Day Lewis a way out of the isolate ego, and, in this sense, it is the symbol of man's deep-seated personal desire for self-transcendence. The magnetic mountain is nothing less than the primordial human community, a pastoral

future. That the ideological hope supersedes and ultimately silences the
intuitive, instinctual drama of the private mind should not prevent us
from recognizing Day Lewis' desire, once again, to keep the two levels
in exact balance. The poem's failure to achieve this balance is a good
index of the age and of the demands it made upon the individual poet.

In this regard, the poem's guiding spirits are significant. Of the four
epigraphs to the four parts, only the first, from Day Lewis' friend Rex
Warner, is explicitly political; and even it celebrates the "Heart's
heyday" in the "movement of masses." The others, from Blake,
Lawrence, and Hopkins, place the emphasis on spiritual as opposed to
social radicalism, or they suggest that the one precedes the other.
Lawrence, in fact, was the guiding spirit to Day Lewis' early "romantic
humanism." In *A Hope for Poetry* Day Lewis confessed, as we have
noted, the strange intermixture of Lawrence and Marx in his attempts
to marry the intuitive and the rational, the private and the public. Yet
he had to admit (as Christopher Caudwell later argued) the irreconcilable conflict of the Lawrencean and the Marxist views—the former
"driven ill and mad, a failure unable to recreate a satisfactory social
group for the nucleus of his own individuality"; the latter offering the
"most whole-hearted attempt ever made to raise the individual to his
highest powers by a conditioning of his environment," yet succumbing
to all the evils of an impersonal and depersonalizing system (47).

The conflict between the two kinds of aspiration—between the old,
which Day Lewis' heart approves, and the new, which fructifies the
imagination; between the idea of a change of heart that should change
society and the idea of a new society which should make a new
man—this conflict should ideally produce the dramatic interplay of a
new poetry. It should be at once responsible to the traditional matter
of poetry (human ideals and aspirations) and to the urgency of the
moment (the practical issues of history):

It is as absurd to tell the poet that he must only feel strongly about
natural scenery as it is to call every "nature-poet" an escapist. Nor is it
right for us to say that the poet should be concerned only with eternal
facts, with summer and winter, birth, marriage and death. These are the
mountain-peaks, the final and everlasting limits of the known world,
but they are always the background against which stand out and are
measured temporal things—the rise and fall of cities, the year's harvest,
the moment's pain. (48)

Christopher Caudwell later argued, in the same vein, for the universal
economic role of poetry. Just as ancient poetry functioned to reconcile

primitive man with his environment, Caudwell claimed, modern poetry must perform a similar function in a technological world.[3] This attempt to explore "eternal" theses—the universal patterns and entities that are the "mountain-peaks" of man's reality—as they are lived in the valleys and urban wastelands of the historical present demands of the poet a conscious, and inevitably forced, adaptation of traditional styles to a new language. The imagery of *The Magnetic Mountain* evinces the stresses and tensions of this kind of poetic metamorphosis, but it also reveals its failures. Still more obtrusive is Day Lewis' reliance on rhetoric and an unsubtle satiric mode to urge his audience toward the new world. A decade later, when translating the *Georgics*, Day Lewis learned the different possibilities for a poetry celebrating nature; but the early 1930's precluded agrarian nostalgia.

The poem's four sections display three basic modes of propaganda: the first details the urgency of action and affirms the existence of the magic mountain; the middle two anatomize the bad faith of the establishment, the "old gang"; and the last explores the continuity leading from the essential past into the essential future. For this "magnetic mountain" Day Lewis speaks of is the embodiment of the basic human drive toward completeness; it exists "Somewhere beyond the railheads/ Of reason" (*Collected Poems*, 82), yet it is "Not where you think but where you are" (110). It is a secular analogue of spiritual rebirth, the change of heart that may proceed either from within outward or oppositely from environment to self. In the act of proclaiming the necessity of the poet as actor, Day Lewis reveals the poet's subordination to society's evolution toward a future.

The thirty-six lyrics composing *The Magnetic Mountain* are thematically continuous but uneven—now exhortative, now analytical, now obstreperously satiric. The satire reveals Day Lewis' basic weakness as a poet, his overwhelming self-seriousness, his forced humor. Part One of the poem, in fact, can never decide whether it is to be a call to arms or an image of the new raised upon the ashes of the old. Day Lewis begins by celebrating his "kestrel joy," his recurrent symbol for the limitless human spirit (and a secular relative of Hopkins' Windhover) now "harried by carrion cares" (81). The "shadow" of "the temporal princes, fear and pain" (82), weigh upon the modern self, and man is condemned in his spiritual poverty to what Lawrence indicated as the Western world's death wish. Thus the appeal of the "magnetic mountain," which rivets "sky to earth," there "Somewhere beyond the railheads/ Of reason." The kestrel alone—the indomitable human spirit, the poetic imagination—may alone "signify the place": "For space stands on its head there/ And time chases its tail" (83).

The first three poems establish the necessity of history's landscape, this world of "iron" that is our modern heritage; they develop the metaphor of the bridge and the journey by which man might hope to rejoin the material with the spiritual. Four shifts the theme, mounting an attack on the old gang with a withering though inappropriate parody based upon the clichés of the bourgeois world. A brief example suffices, for it speaks eloquently of the emotional commitment Day Lewis had made:

> You can't go further along these lines;
> Positively this is the end of the track;
> It's rather late and there's no train back.
> So if you are wanting to get anywhere
> You must use your feet or take to the air,
> The penny-a-liner, the seven-course-diner,
> Prebendary Cute and the water-diviner . . .(84)

But the first order of business of him who would depart for the mountain is to "take a light engine back along the line/ For a last excursion . . . " (84). Again and again, a latent nostalgia creeps to the surface, to be forcibly suppressed; until the poet must at least admit that his conveyance to the new world—that is, the new self he must make before he achieves the mountain—must have the "old world's best in her ribs and ballast" (111). No matter what the radical mixture of metaphors, the future is never far from the enduring past. The mountain signifies the essential purity of every heart, past or future.

Parts Two and Three, however, are devoted to exposing the hypocrisy and moral evasions of the "old gang." The two sections parade forth respectively *Four Defendants* and *Four Enemies*: the first, defenders of the status quo; the second, enemies of the kestrel spirit of the revolution. Each of the two sections develops by alternating lyrics: the First Defendant speaks, to be answered by the poet; then the Second Defendant, and so on. The defendants represent in order the aristocracy, the politicians, the clergy, and the bourgeois family. The four enemies of Part Three incorporate the lure of the flesh (and its associations of moral guilt), the appeal of bourgeois practical morality, the faith in positivistic science, and estheticism (or the uncommitted poet). Although each defendant and each enemy is heard and refuted, there is neither a drama of ideas nor one of style; the conclusion to each part is preordained by the poet's commitment:

> While oaks of pedigree
> Stand over a rich seam,
> Another sinks the shaft,
> Fills furnace, gets up steam.
>
> These never would break through
> The orbit of their year,
> Admit no altered stress,
> Decline a change of gear.
>
> The tree grips soil, the bird
> Knows how to use the wind;
> But the full man must live
> Rooted yet unconfined. (96)

Having tried and condemned those who "take the bribe," the poet is ready for action: "It is now or never, the hour of the knife,/ The break with the past, the major operation" (107). But Part Four is more declamatory than dramatic; "the west is . . . in flames" (108), and the poem is caught between its desire to linger upon that destruction and its responsibility for celebrating the world to come. Between the two, it performs neither adequately nor convincingly; the poet merely details the sacrifice attendant upon the change of heart:

> You who would come with us,
> Think what you stand to lose—
> An assured income, the will
> In your favour and the feel
> Of firmness underfoot. (112)

And yet, in some way the "firmness underfoot," the "Props of an English scene" (113) will not let go; and the poet is left in the end where he was in *Transitional Poem*: committed to an action to follow, celebrating the poet as the first architect of vision, who constitutes the magnetic mountain. The poem's conclusion returns to that tenacious religious strain that Day Lewis later detected as having always been a part of his temperament. There is perhaps no better example of the confusion of the times than that it forced the collapsing of ideological hope and religious consolations. A surrogate absolute was needed to replace the authority that had disappeared from the center of modern life and from the English poetic tradition, and that surrogate proved not so much to be a new ideology as a new admixture of the old.

The Magnetic Mountain confirmed the shared purposes and even the essential style of the leftist poets of the 1930's, who composed a "movement," not because they were poets of like sensibility, but because the age provoked conscientious men to similar sentiments. And the era also provoked poets to reassess their role, not only with regard to tradition, but also in terms of a nebulous and hypothetical future. Day Lewis later observed that they "had in common, apart from the climate of our times . . . a certain shared basis of thought": the recognition, as Michael Roberts put it, "that oneself is no more important than a flower in a field."[4] This attitude toward the limited self is a conviction grown out of Eliot's explorations of the ingrown ego and his protestations against personality in poetry. But the aptness of Eliot's stance had to be tested in a decade in which immediate historical and political chaos manifested the consequences of spiritual malaise—in which tradition and the church no longer provided the communal center for an orderly life. The individual personality, deprived of its Romantic identity, was similarly bereft of the communal solidarity of society. As a result, a new community, a revived system, was imperative if the isolated self were to survive. Some "magic mountain" was necessary—some manifestation of optimum hope. Toward that end, poetry had to assume a social conscience—a religious poetry circumscribed by secular ends.

CHAPTER 4

The End of Ideology

"IN A tricky, darkening decade we were a generation which had not vision equal to desire"—thus Day Lewis reflects on the deficiencies of himself and his contemporaries who discovered that, contrary to the nature of the tradition in which they were raised, action must precede idea (*Buried Day*, 217). Two years after the publication of *The Magnetic Mountain* he had given up his teaching job at Cheltenham to make a career as free-lance writer. During those two years he had become increasingly a political activist; but by his own admission, his activities were motivated more by emotion than reason. His Marxism, as he repeatedly admitted, was sentimental and nostalgic, and it had a definite "religious quality" (209). His was a mind, he noted, "quite incompatible . . . with the materialism and rigidity of Communist doctrines" (211); for his own materialism was not so rigid nor so absolute.

Unlike such Cambridge activists as John Cornford, Day Lewis was unwilling to forgo the perquisites of his literary tradition and hence to subordinate his art to the revolutionary social will. Christopher Caudwell, the only leftist critic in England capable of speaking convincingly about the role of art within Communist society, has emphasized the divided loyalties that claimed these poets. Writing at the time Day Lewis, Auden, and Spender were most fully engaged in their separate roles as activist poets, Caudwell analyzed the poet's responsibility to write out of his life and also the inevitable "bourgeois" tendency of would-be Marxist poets to divide their art from conscience and hence preserve art in and for itself. The bourgeois radicals, he insisted,

announce themselves as prepared to merge with the proletariat, to accept its theory and its organisation, in every field of concrete living except that of art. Now this reservation—unimportant to the ordinary man—is absolutely disastrous for the artist, precisely because his most

important function is to be an artist. It leads to a gradual separation
between his living and his art. . . . His proletarian living bursts into his
art in the form of crude and grotesque scraps of Marxist phraseology
and the mechanical application of the living proletarian theory. . . . His
bourgeois art bursts into his proletarian living in the form of
extraordinary and quite unnecessary outbursts of bourgeois inde-
pendence and indiscipline or quite apparent bourgeois distortions of
poetry's revolutionary theory.[1]

Caudwell, who was speaking in direct response to the "Auden
Group," no doubt had in mind works like Day Lewis' *A Hope for
Poetry* and the journal comments of Spender which led in 1936 to
publication of *The Destructive Element*. For the recurrent schizo-
phrenia of most apologies for poetry in the 1930's was, as Caudwell
observed, the incompatible argument that the poet must be socially and
politically engaged but that his first loyalties must be to his craft. In the
whole of the Marxist economy, this was just another instance of
bourgeois dualism, a reflection of the more metaphysical concern of
how to maintain individuality within the collective society. As Day
Lewis admitted in *Buried Day*, everywhere "D. H. Lawrence got mixed
into my Marxism" (210); and Lawrence was Caudwell's example of the
rebel who recognized the evils of the bourgeois state but could offer
only a "Fascist" or anarchist solution. His was the error of seeking
"salvation through the free act of the individual will amid decay and
disaster."[2]

More directly to the point, Caudwell isolated not only Day Lewis'
problem but the very theme out of which his poetry in the mid- and
late 1930's grew. The old unreconciled dilemma of *Transitional
Poem* —the divided self—was now projected outward into the actualities
of social events and his involvement in them. As Day Lewis succinctly
stated in *A Hope for Poetry*, "Standing at the end of an epoch, the
poet's arms are stretched out in opposite poles, the old life and the
new; that is his power and his crucifixion" (48). Indeed, his poem
"Johnny Head-in-Air" later employed that very metaphor of the poet
as secular Christ (*Collected Poems*, 132).

I   *Knowledge of Necessity*

In *A Time to Dance*, which appeared in 1935, two titles, "The
Conflict" and "In Me Two Worlds," signify not only two overtly
political poems but provide explicit metaphors for the deep-seated
division of personal loyalties that characterizes bourgeois Leftist

poetry in the 1930's. Guilt, strangely enough, the very thing communal involvement is supposed to resolve, is the animating force. How to be concurrently an activist and a poet, how to reconcile the civic with the esthetic, was Day Lewis' burden. Propagandist activity in publications like *New Country* and the *Left Review*, appearances at public meetings, activist lectures, even party membership—these actions did not exactly suffice, especially as an answer for the poet's responsibility, first of all, to his craft. This division pervades Day Lewis' and Spender's musings on poetics and ideology, and Caudwell correctly identified their desire to commit everything but their artistic individuality to the movement as another instance of Romantic self-deception. Day Lewis, who in fact recognized this difficulty at crucial times, made it the emotional center of some of his best work. Thus we have the guilt and also the search for a style that might move poetry toward action: not as propaganda or rhetoric but as a voice of the heroic future; not a poetry forecasting magnetic mountains but one evoking their immanent presence concealed in the chaos of history.

In a sense, we might say Day Lewis was searching for his own true style. Other than the sequence called "Overtures to Death" and two well-known short lyrics, "Bombers" and "Newsreel," his only two pieces of any originality written during the period between 1933 and 1940 are narrative sequences: one, the flight-to-Australie sections of "A Time to Dance"; the other, "The Nabara," based on a storied incident of the Spanish Civil War. These poems of narrative action, which are, ironically, nonpolitical, eschew abstraction and the philosophical base of the earlier long poems; above all, since they are not allegorical, they do not subordinate narrative to a moral or symbolic purpose, though they were conceived as exempla of heroic action and sacrifice. These poems focus on the flesh and blood of man's little heroics, orchestrating as it were the rhythms of an action; and, with quiet eloquence, they affirm the possibility of a successful action and heroism in an antiheroic time. If the action they orchestrate is a kind of communal action, it is not an advertisement of Communism in the abstract but a celebration of man's purposefulness and the strength of united action: his will to endure, the little heroics of his sacrifices, and, above all, his recurrent struggle with the forces of his environment, both natural and social, which constitute his necessity. Although we will discuss later the latent sentimentalism of these poems, it suffices to say here that Day Lewis sets this narrative style against the lyrics of guilt as he sets the instinct of hope against conscious despair in a dialogue which seeks to join the isolated self with the struggling society. Above all, the poet's problem was to recognize and realize the maxim of Engels, "Freedom is the knowledge of necessity."

In his essay on Lawrence, Caudwell makes a point about the essential traditionalism of a Marxist esthetic. Speaking of two errant directions of the bourgeois artist—either his conformity to the system, making his product commercial; or his revolt from the system, into art for art's sake—Caudwell remarks on the extreme individualism of the latter in its betrayal of the essential social activity of communication which for him is the true role of poetry: "The social values inherent in the art form, such as syntax, tradition, rules, techniques, form, accepted tonal scale, now seem to have little value, for the art work more and more exists for the individual alone. The art work is necessarily always the product of a tension between old conscious social formulations—the art 'form'—and new individual experience made conscious—the art 'content' or the artist's 'message.' "[3] Disregarding the logical muddle, not to say the bias that prevents Caudwell from seeing that this argument is essentially a latter-day Georgian one against the experimentalism of the 1920's, we may observe the clutch of tradition that denies to art the revolution urged upon the state. The explicit form-content dichotomy suggests that Marxist art should only pour new wine into old bottles. The strange case of Julian Bell, calling for a revolutionary poetry which spoke in the plain, clear, rhetorical style of Pope, is an apposite case in point: for Bell and Caudwell were ideologically far apart except about where the poet must find his forms. The proletarian audience could only respond to a traditional style, not to an experimental (hence, private) style. Ironically, Caudwell would not consider these "social values" as conventions manifesting the aristocratic tradition of poetry. Because history was inevitable, the past had been right for its time. Revolution dialectically incorporated the past, including its art forms. And besides, all art had its origin in the primitive relationship between man and his environment. These paradoxes troubled Day Lewis who was seeking at once a new language, a revolutionary voice, and a solid poetics that only tradition could provide. The unresolved tensions of his poems during this period—and, occasionally, some of his better effects—are the result.

We have but to look at the group of short lyrics which preface the long title piece of *A Time to Dance* to find his essential theme: the need to rejuvenate the tradition. The second, for example, entitled "Moving In" (*Collected Poems,* 126), stems from reflections upon the poet's establishing himself in a new residence, that archetypal change-of-home experience which had haunted his childhood.

The poem begins with a question and with deftness explores the possibilities of the situation:

Is it your hope, hope's heath, heart's home, here at the lane's end?
Deeds are signed, structure is sound though century-old;
Redecorated throughout, all modern conveniences, the cable extended;
Need grope no more in corners nor cower from dark and cold.

The division and directness are counterpointed by Audenesque ellipses and by the indirect address; the analogical meanings thrust themselves forward. Anglo-Saxon echoes reinforce the house's ancient foundation, for the house is as pointed by symbol as E. M. Forster's *Howards End*: it is England; it is tradition. And his "moving-in" is the nostalgic return to the past, to the warmth, comfort, and security to which he is still tied by the umbilical cable. Yet it is also the newcomers' hope that, in returning to the past, they will be made whole—they who stand, though not so despairing as Matthew Arnold, between "two worlds," dreaming of contact with both. The house, then, is memory, and it embodies those old and familiar antitheses: passion and pain, hope and fear, the secure past and the indeterminate future. The house is located somewhere between the country and the town, a retreat, a kind of freedom that is achieved only in his consciousness of necessity: "No private good will let you forget all/ Those, time's accessories. . . . "

And so Day Lewis returns to the only possible source for poetry. If the social conflict is not reflected in the personal, it is not authentic, or cannot be authentically rendered. He admitted what Caudwell called his bourgeois confusions, which ironically were the very sources of his poetic vitality. "In Me Two Worlds" (129) is as private a public poem as the decade produced, an explicit metaphor for the two worlds which necessity freed the man of conscience to inhabit: "The moving point of dust/ Where past and future meet. . . . " "The Conflict" (127), as another title indicates, is the life and the death of the self, pulled one way by its own natural tropism toward the past, and the other way by its sense of moral decency toward the anticipation of a new life. His "singing" brings him momentary, but not permanent, peace:

> Yet living here,
> As one between two massing powers I live
> Whom neutrality cannot save
> Nor occupation cheer.

That the poem dissolves into a rather patent cry in behalf of the "red advance of life" is to be expected, if not approved. But the real subject is the singer's dilemma in this "no man's land," where his singing is neither action for suffering, except that it conditions the self to wait and to deny its essential selfhood.

The volume's opening poem, "Learning to Talk" (125)—exploiting the metaphor of the child's struggle toward articulation and hence identity—makes clear the paradox that animates the volume. Learning to talk, to be the voice of the masses, is an act of self-sacrifice. The process of learning is that of exchanging one self (private ego) for another (social self); the gain is in the loss. To move toward articulation is to forfeit the child's innocence and hence to come to a knowledge of necessity. Committed to history as process, not to say as dialectic, the poet learns to talk in the present of a world which cannot be realized for his present self:

> Though we fall once, though we often,
> Though we fall to rise not again,
> From our horizons sons begin;
> When we go down, they will be tall ones.

History is a drama of fathers sacrificed to the dream of sons.

Otherwise, *A Time to Dance* consists of aggressive counterattacks against the inner voice of nostalgia: "A Warning to Those Who Live on Mountains" (131), the intellectual elite, the uncommitted idealists; or laments for "Losers" (128), the sacrificial proles; or the Audenesque ballad of "Johnny Head-in-Air" (132), a return to the journey metaphor, man led to the crossroads where he must either "take the bribe" or make the right choice of the "cryptic way." The poet is impaled on the cross of his divided self. And finally, we have the delicate, tasteful little lyric, "The Ecstatic" (137), which evidences Day Lewis' true style, one emerging from a sensitive, unforced response to the harmonies of nature. Unfortunately, this kind of poem he had little time for; for it fixes his sympathies in an earlier time and close to the Romantic vision.

The title poem (141), however, dominates *A Time to Dance* and provides the best index of the divisions that lacerated Day Lewis: the guilt, the sense of impotence and frustration, the resurgent hopes, above all the irrational will to find the better in the worse—all instances of what Caudwell had pointed to as sentiments of the bourgeois poet moving among an adopted proletariat. "A Time to Dance," which has an interesting history, when first published ran 763 lines, more than 250 of which (everything after the elegiac section) were quickly discarded, though some few small sections reappear in the *Collected*

Poems as "Songs," or better, as satiric parodies: for instance, "A Carol" (140), beginning "Oh hush thee my baby,/ Thy cradle's in pawn"; or the well-known parody of Christopher Marlowe, "Come live with me and be my love,/ And we will all the pleasures prove/ Of peace and plenty, bed and board,/ That chance employment may afford" (139). The shortened version, as Day Lewis insisted, attempts to eliminate the more overtly propagandistic elements of a poem which, after all, was begun as an elegy. Indeed, the poem's divided allegiances comprehend the whole range of Day Lewis' talent and its limitations.

Stimulated by the premature and unexpected death of his friend L. P. Hedges, the poem begins as an elegy that is not a lament but rather a tribute to Hedges' vital and stimulating mind. Hedges, dead to the world, must be made to live in the poet's song—as stimulus of the dance against (not of) death. The longest and most substantial section of the poem is, therefore, a verse retelling of the flight to Australia: "Sing we the two lieutenants, Parer and M'Intosh,/ After the war, wishing to hie them home to Australia." The flight, made in 1920 in an obsolete, condemned aircraft by two Australian flyers who had fought in World War I, had entered the annals of English subheroics. Day Lewis' particular use of the experience stresses the ordinary virtues of tenacity and ingenuity of man's struggle with his environment and the laws of necessity and reifies also the marginal heroism and the triumphant brotherhood of the two lieutenants. The explicit purpose of the celebration, of action in the face of death, is to orchestrate the dance and thus to pay homage to Hedges, the embodiment of life will prematurely cut off in a spiritless age. Day Lewis does not simply wish to insist on a "happy end," by way of ignoring the reality of Hedges' death; on the contrary, his mood, grabbing hope from the clutches of despair, is well within the elegiac tradition. But, more important, he wished to elevate action into a symbol of human endurance and to celebrate it as a manifestation of man's denial of his alienation.

The flyers transcend hardship only by submitting to it, and they succeed in their journey by following no "average law." The journey of the two men is homeward, a compact of brotherhood against the divisiveness and the adversity of war, a triumph that exploits danger. The flight, then, is a metaphor of man's self-sustaining hope and also an instance of a communal action leading to successful reunion. The plane's "obsolete design" is like tradition, a tenuous vehicle but the only available means of transport. Like the weather which recurrently threatens and the alien landscape which offers little sustenance and comfort, the flight is a condition of necessity which drives one to communal action. And the action, like an epic journey, is homeward, the desire of the poet. But the poem asserts the allegory only in the larger context. Day Lewis' limited triumph within this mode—which reflects a nostalgia for the epic line—is that he keeps his focus on the epical particulars of an action, at no little sacrifice to lyricism and eloquence. His long line, an epic imitation, fails to translate the contemporary event into the mythical action. Thus the heroics it presumes to orchestrate never transcend the event and do not survive the occasion.

But "A Time to Dance," in its original version,[4] is not all orchestrated heroics. Of the nine sections, the two longest are the narrative of the flight and the elegy proper (sections three and four, comprising more than four hundred lines). What follows the elegy is more rhetoric than song, a counterpointing of Hedges' indomitable will and infectious human sympathy with the age that has destroyed these virtues. Now angry, now propagandistic, now cleverly satiric, now crudely bombastic, these concluding sections draw out the analogy between the inspiration the poet draws from Hedges' death and the comfort the masses should extract from their suffering and dying fellows. Day Lewis thus integrates personal and public themes: the flight toward new worlds, premised on Engels' *"Freedom is knowledge of necessity"* (*Time to Dance,* 57); and the triumph of self-sacrifice in communal action.

Of course, the poem does not hang together; it is a dance of differences, of events and styles, seeking a "home" or relation. The narrative flight section, while it instances one of Day Lewis' more accomplished modes, seems more an evasion of the reality of Hedges' death than an analogue of its true significance. The elegy, on the other hand, lurches between personal lament and willed affirmation: "He was our dynamo, our warmth, our beam/ Transmitter of mirth—it is a town's collapse/ Not easily repaired" (*Time to Dance,* 46). In the end, the example of the flight is reduced to its "lesson," to the masses of men: "It is using the currents of air to waft your wings/ And adverse ranges for test of climbing-speed" (*Time to Dance,* 57). But the real urgency that breaks over the poem and into the heartfelt mood of the elegy is the anger of the parodies and the inept (not to say, inapt) intrusion of the verses beginning, "Yes, why do we all, seeing a Red, feel small?"—a poem which Day Lewis had previously published in the *Left Review,* one destined to cause him much embarrassment. The elimination of all but the coda following the elegy does not entirely restore the poem's integrity, but it does indicate its true center. For the death-rebirth motif, suffering transcending itself in action, allows the progression from personal loss to social vision:

> In my heart's mourning underworld I say
> As miner's entombed singing despair to sleep . . .
> For I knew at last, wholly accepting death,
> Though earth had taken his body and air his breath,
> He was not in heaven or earth: he was in me.
>
> .   .   .   .   .
>
> For my friend that was dead is alive. He bore transplanting
> Into common soil. Strongly he grows
> Upon the heart and gives the tentative wing
> Take-off for flights, surety for repose. (*Time to Dance*, 48)

The bourgeois sentiments—"a dance in spite/ Of death: love, the affirmative in all living" (48)—are modulated into the dialectical hope of masses moving and of a world evolving:

> Then a leviathan, breaking the surface of
> Terrified seas, a more than continent
> Shall arise—a world shaking off its back
> The abyss and waste welter of multitudinous
> Oppressing, drying its valleys in the sunlight,
> Reaching for heaven with firm and ardent hills . . .
>   Sirs, you are that world
> Shall make a new world and be all the world. (58)

But the one tone betrays the other; sententiousness and sentiment go hand in hand. At the very end, the poem can only urge sacrifice to necessity, and, from the welter of human sufferers ("in the machine's heart") "feel their generous heat" (64).

II *Murky Waters*

The unevenness of "A Time to Dance"—its impossible struggle to reconcile the sentiments of elegy with the rhetoric of hope—bespeaks the divisive pressures which possessed Day Lewis when he chose to retire from teaching and withdrew exclusively to write. They are even more evident in his next major effort, *Noah and the Waters* (1936), an abortive drama "begun as the 'book' for a choral ballet" which, according to the author, turned out to be "something in the tradition of the medieval morality plays."[5] In view of the result, this statement is my no means convincing. Yet the fact that Day Lewis identified his

effort with that faded genre reveals at least one dimension of his
purpose: the moral high dudgeon that usurps the art and violates the
biblical metaphor on which the "play" is presumably based. The result
is unfortunate, especially since the Prologue and opening Chorus
contain some very fine lines: a delicately worked out allegory based on
the Noah myth which Day Lewis had used with effectiveness as early as
Transitional Poem. But *Noah and the Waters* is possessed by the terms
of its Epigraph, from the *Communist Manifesto*: "Finally, when the
class war is about to be fought to a finish, disintegration of the ruling
class and the old order of society becomes so active, so acute, that a
small part of the ruling class breaks away to make common cause with
the revolutionary class, the class which holds the future in its
hands. . . . "

The play takes this declaration as gospel but turns it neatly into Day
Lewis' recurring concern with the continuity of tradition. Noah, the
sensibility of the old order, is a member of the ruling bourgeoisie
disturbed by the course of history and by the impasse of the present.
He is man caught, once again, between past and future, bourgeois and
proletariat, the stagnant pools of self-interest and the flowing waters of
necessary change. A member of the ruling Burgesses, he is drawn to the
waters of change; that is to say, he is conscious of the dialectic's
inevitability, and he is conscience itself. His dilemma is manifest by the
Two Voices, the divisions of his inner self: the one, his death will,
counsels submission to necessity, inaction, and escape; the other, his life
will, advises action and commitment to the urgency of change. The play
is deficient not so much because of the allegorical terms as because it
fails to translate them into either action or poetry.

The drama proper, such as it is, is a contest for Noah's soul
between the rebel Waters and the ruling Burgesses—a contest also
reflected within Noah by the contrasting Two Voices. In the debate
which is conducted in obvious terms, the Waters, in revolt, call for
release from the status quo—from the stagnation of subservience to
Burgess rule and from the industrial state. And the Burgesses respond in
the clichés of bourgeois liberalism: they will make the necessary minor
improvements but also preserve things as they are. So proceed the
various debates toward their inevitable end: Noah, refusing to "take the
bribe," opts for his life will and the future of the flowing waters; the
Waters rise in revolt to inundate the Burgesses who helplessly retreat
into their illusions and accrued securities. The play progresses inexorably away from the lyrical resonances of the Prologue and Chorus
toward the propagandistic tones of its governing terms. The debates,

especially those between the Burgesses and Noah, reflect something of the harshness of Eliot's Knights in the second half of *Murder in the Cathedral* (one of the possible models for the play), but without the contextual aptness of the Knights' apologetic pandering. And, unlike its other possible models—the psycho-political dramas of Auden and Isherwood—*Noah and the Waters* fails to admit and hence to dramatize the mysterious but powerful instinctual forces attendant upon a choice like Noah's, the choice of breaking away.

The "play's" lapses are all the worse because of its promising beginning. Day Lewis' exclusion of all but the Prologue and two of the choral passages from his *Collected Poems* indicates well enough what parts of the play survived its occasion. The Prologue and the First Chorus form a kind of modern prospect poem, a love song to the enduring land that is the corporeal spirit of a people's progressive history: "Stand with us here," the Chorus sings,

> Feel underfoot the linked vertebrae of your land
> Stretching north to the far fells, the head of rivers.
> Prehistory sleeps below in many beds. Before
> Man set a value on his thoughts or made a prison for fear,
> These hills were grown up, to the sky happily married . . . (162)

The choral lyrics are filled with the sense of history as substance, as the ground of Time (the "curve of ploughland" that is a "graph of history"). They lament man's historical alienation (hence his fall) from this primordial ground and his withdrawal to the bourgeois town. The movement is, in effect, from organic space to mechanical time. Modern man's image is the town, which perpetually exploits the plowshare. (This country-town contrast, despite its obvious immediate relevance and its aptness to Marxian distinctions, belongs to the pastoral nostalgia of the English poetic tradition.) "Noah, figure of your fate," must either join with the waters that will sweep away the town or be inundated by them. But what follows this Chorus fails to connect the rejuvenating force of the "curve of ploughland" with the modern crisis, which seems less spiritual than immediately political. The play goes astray precisely because it moves toward the fixed terms of allegory and away from the problematics of action. An ideologically committed morality play is destined to be static, even if its ideological structure is dialectical.

Noah and the Waters, a symptomatic leftist poem, begins as art and ends as propaganda. The very idea of writing a "choral ballet," or even a "morality play," indicates that Day Lewis, like Eliot, aspired toward a more public form than lyric poetry could provide. His brief career as a novelist, which began at about the same time, evidences a similar purpose. In an essay written about this time and published first in the *Left Review*,[6] Day Lewis addressed himself to the causes and consequences of modern poetry's unpopularity—its abstractness and strategic obscurantism. One historical reason, he suggested, is the decline of the oral lyrical tradition, which set the poet among his auditors as a person and actor. His is no doubt too simple a rationalization (though he would cling to it in one or more of its possible forms from *A Hope for Poetry* to *The Lyric Impulse*), but it answers for at least two of the characteristic directions his poetry took, or sought to take, in the middle and late 1930's. In the first place, it accords with the Marxist demand that the poet return to the living language of the proletariat and that he turn his verse into the spiritual analogue of the masses' action. If he cannot become a minstrel, he must then find some equally public marriage of poetry and action—in drama, for example. On the other hand, this rejection of isolated selfhood and of the language of the personal, interior life commands the poet first of all to create a poetic camaraderie (and, in fact, a poetic society) that is an analogue of the true communal society of the future. In *A Hope for Poetry*, to underscore a crucial passage quoted earlier, he put it directly: "We shall not begin to understand post-war poetry until we realize that the poet is appealing above all for the creation of a society in which the real and living contact between man and man may again become possible. That is why, speaking from the living unit of himself and his friends, he appeals for the contraction of the social group to a size at which human contact may again be established and demands the destruction of all the impediments to love" (38).

The contradictions are self-evident. Calling on the one hand for a retreat from the obscurantism and the in-group knowledge that characterized modernism, it rationalized the very kind of coterie poetry—with its private language, inside jokes, and arcane brotherhood—which Auden and his contemporaries often affected: the boy-scout group waging its campaigns in the public-school world of betrayal and mystery. By the mid-1930's Day Lewis had exhausted the possibilities which this language held out for him, largely because it was an adopted and not a natural style. The "lyric impulse" sought to reclaim his first allegiance; and the lyrical, he admitted, could not be separated from a "certain irresponsibility" (*Hope for Poetry*, 67). The lyric impulse was in contest with social urgencies. And the love ethic—"We must love one another or die," Auden's now-suppressed line put it—was forced to lie down with revolutionary violence. *Noah and the Waters* was the immediate product of Day Lewis' need to discover a publicly influential, not simply a publicly available, style. But it was, to say the least, pathetic—in no sense the equal of his narrative poems in finding the ear of the general reader.

III *Overtures to Death*

Noah, however, proved in its failure to be a crucial point in Day Lewis' career: the shock of recognition that his political activism had exacted from him an enormous price in poetic energy and concentration. Edwin Muir's review of the work, Day Lewis said, made him at last aware that poetry and public-spiritedness must necessarily be incompatible. In *The Buried Day,* he records the epiphanic moment when, speaking before an anti-Fascist rally of artists, he first sensed the self-indulgence and illegitimate pleasures of the public man holding power over an audience (222–23). But his withdrawal from activism was, he observed, neither sudden nor absolute; it had begun, in fact, with his retirement from teaching which, though it freed him from institutional restraints upon political activity, also made him more conscious of the writer's exclusive realm of experience—the self.

The poetry written immediately after *Noah*, while in no sense a radical departure from the "romantic humanism" that had determined his Communist sympathies, began to confront the reality of the communal ideal from a new perspective. If Marx destroyed the principle of metaphysical evil and the Christian doctrine of grace, his absorption of the individual self into the dialectical processes of history provided a kind of secular surrogate for grace. Committed absolutely to history, the Communist was spared no less than the Christian the agony of nothingness and the meaninglessness of death. The inevitability of revolution—not to say the basic principle that all human action is an exercise of force—portended violence and death in the process of events. The Marxist teleology, however, resolved violence and rejected sentimental death even as it made action the equivalent of life, the inexorable process of becoming. The bourgeois obsession with individual death was a manifestation of the bourgeois illusion; the Christian's transcendent future, evidence of the bourgeois death will. Marxist violence was the means of history and the prelude to the millennium.

By 1936, the clashing ideologies of bourgeois violence (to preserve the status quo) and revolutionary violence (leading to dialectical change) had become a fact of history that bloodied the Spanish earth.

To Day Lewis, secluded in his home, the reality was at once distant and immediate. The guilt attendant upon his choice to remain physically, if not intellectually, inactive leaves a distinct mark on his poetry. But, what is more important, the fact of death as an inescapable individual event and as a product of impersonal violence came more and more to the center of his meditations. The death of his father in 1937, the crystallizing event, led directly to the ambitious "Overtures to Death" in which he achieved (for the first time since *From Feathers to Iron*) the essential balance between personal and public reality of experience. But the entire volume to which the poem lends its title is death-centered and violence-ridden, the meaning of which is not to be resolved by appeal to ideological explanation. The quiet at Musbury, now his home, brought the experience of death and violence more immediately before him than ever, as the inescapable fact of his consciousness.

Overtures to Death (1938) is dedicated interestingly to E. M. Forster—a testimony, perhaps, to the kind of Bloomsbury humanism to which Day Lewis' radical sentiments had retreated but, more probably, to the deeply implanted sense of English history and the strength of its rural laborers and yeoman stock which had become, as it were, his proletariat. The shorter poems of this volume, significantly, divide almost evenly between rurally inspired meditations and observations about the violence of modern history. Of the latter, "Bombers" and "Newsreel" have become anthology regulars, their style an exemplum of the modern poet's ability to transform the contemporary landscape into effective poetic language. The rural poems seem so alien to their age it is easy to overlook that they point to the future directions of Day Lewis' work.

There are "Spring Song" and "Night Piece," "The Three Cloud Maidens," "Behold the Swan," and the most indicative title of all, "Passage from Childhood"—each a delicately turned lyric, poems without any design upon the reader, with echoes of that Georgian pastoral which inspired Day Lewis' first poems. Collectively, the poems are of an idle mind in the best sense of the phrase—poems emerging from the mind's release from time and the perturbations of immediate history. Perhaps for this reason they invariably reflect the child in nature—that is, nature as a metaphor of the child's mind, the indivisible harmony of the two, the prelapsarian moment that still exists vestigially at the mind's interior borders. "Passage from Childhood' (205) incorporates the nostalgic resonances of this experience, reflecting as it does almost exactly the same metaphysical situation as Frost's "Directive," which appeared a full decade later:

His earliest memory, the mood
Fingered and frail as maidenhair,
Was this—the china cup somewhere
In a green deep wood.

The pristine world now lost, existing only at the edge of memory, is aptly embodied in the image of the "china cup," the redemptive grail in a sacred wood. (The Freudian intimations effectively reinforce this "memory.") The passage from childhood, in short, is inevitable: from innocence, from the womb, from unity. But passage *from* is also a passage *to*: to imaginative adventure, the mind's journey into itself. The poem sensitively explores this introspective act, the "exile" journey into the alien landscape of the self where alone exists the sacred wood and the redemptive grail. It is a poem in search of the "buried Day Lewis," to employ the pun in the title of his autobiography. Like Day Lewis' other uses of nature, the poem is a metaphor of the poet's creative act, to which his first drinking of the cup (a sacramental pact with the ideal) condemns him:

He's one more ghost, engaged to keep
Eternity's long hours and mewed
Up in live flesh with no escape
From solitude.

This kind of commitment, which transcends all the external obligations of the public man, is the authentic voice of the poet discovering himself. But, in a very real sense, Day Lewis' more public poems, at their best, simply focus on the other side of the same theme: human strategies of self-evasion, the crippling illusions of bourgeois life, the modern paralysis of will, and, above all, the death wish evident in man's refusal to make an inward journey, to know himself. "Newsreel" (171), for example, directs its attention outward from the poet's self upon a world that refuses to turn inward, except into its collective illusions. The poem's scene is as apt as it is conventional: the movie theater is an inner space, like that of the self, turned into a tomb. Offering images of reality, the theater provides the viewers a false refuge from the truth of images—"Enter the dream-house . . . leaving/ Your debts asleep, your history at the door"—and hence allows them to deny the reality of history's events. Turning fact into appearance, the viewers, in a "womb-deep sleep," can ignore the appearance of violence. Their retreat inward is not, like the child's or poet's, redemptive but escapist. The poem does more, obviously, than expose the futureless-ness of illusions; it exposes the individual dream that the self is innocent of history. Poetry, to the contrary, must be a re-inversion of this inverted image, a mirror mirroring the mirror.

In a slightly different vein, "Bombers" (170) sets two images in reverberating opposition: the one, nature's bursting seed, identified with the child's fertile innocence; the other, the death-pregnant bombers, the inverted anima-mother, "wombs that ache to be rid of death." Like "Newsreel," this kind of poem, setting appearance against reality, cannot avoid the rhetorical ending:

> Choose between your child and this full embryo.
> Shall your guilt bear arms, and the children you want
> Be condemned to die by the powers you pant for
> And haunt the houses you never built.

To choose the "child" is to exercise the life will in the face of the death will, to opt for the organic as opposed to the mechanical principle, to regain a world in which appearance and reality are one.

The conditions of this choice, in the present moment of history, are the subject of two very different kinds of poems which dominate the volume: "The Nabara" and "Overtures to Death." "The Nabara" (191), the second of Day Lewis' poetic narratives, is like its predecessor an attempt to orchestrate heroics—in this case, of self-sacrifice. Based on the account in G. L. Steer's *The Tree of Gernika* of a battle between a larger Fascist cruiser and four government trawlers which were escorts to an arms ship bringing supplies to the fighting Basques, the poem celebrates the act of communal sacrifice and the transcendent strength of communal action. Employing epic conventions, tempered for a less heroic age, and a neo-Virgilian line, the poem holds eloquently, unpretentiously, and undogmatically to the minutiae of an action—but an action so far removed (by the flatness of its poetry, not to say from the poet's direct experience) from the violent occasion as to appear to be neither epic in quality nor realistic in content. In short, trying to avoid sentimentality by fixing on the discrete particulars of the event, Day Lewis falls into another kind of sentimentality, demanding too much of a "storied" event. That the *Nabara* episode was only a minor incident in the larger history of the war is just the point—it is the norm of modern heroics—the sacrificial human action made in the faith that history will serve man if he serves it. The heroes are not ideologues, not self-conscious; they are their ship.

But the poet *is* self-conscious, and the Basques ultimately become their symbolic act: "For these I have told of," the poem ends, "freedom was flesh and blood." The role of the poem is to celebrate the immortality of sacrificial action. "In the rudeness of their heart to die rather than surrender"—this overture modern man must make to death in order to make it an instrument of his freedom not in the sense of the death will but as a force that moves him to deny the living death of inaction. "Overtures to Death" (178) offers a philosophical variation on the theme.

The unique quality of "Overtures to Death," a poem of nearly three hundred lines in seven distinct lyrics, is that more than half of its individual poems employ a ballad quatrain, a form Auden had revived and adapted to a satiric mode. With Auden, the ballad form usually returns to its traditional anecdotal line and to that sense of a human action in a mysterious landscape anterior to history—and it thus becomes appropriate for metaphysical and psychological themes. But Auden's subject was the malaise of his age, the absurdity of its scientific, spiritual, moral quests. In adapting the ballad form to satiric ends—for example, in "The Ballad of Miss Edith Gee"—he married folk form with a sophisticated mode, but, at the same time, preserved himself from the somber rhetoric his stance might otherwise have demanded. Day Lewis' talent is by no means so resourceful as Auden's in its use of the form. In the case of "Overtures to Death," the poem offers distance from the starkness of its subject; but more important, it places the meditations in a context at once timeless and immediate. For Day Lewis' subject is the uses of death in a history that is producing more and more of it less and less naturally.

The poem's seven sections move from bourgeois to proletarian death: from a world which tries to shut out the fact by containing it in forms of transcendence to a world which must condition its very actions to the omnipresence and inevitability of the fact. The one evidences the death will; the other, the life will. As such, the poem celebrates the transformation of the self that is born into one world and thrust rudely into the necessity of the other. It is another reprise (at once satiric and direct) on Day Lewis' perennial theme.

The initial poem explores the world of the fledgling self, the world of bourgeois death:

> You [death] were the one our parents
> Could not forget or forgive
> A remittance man, a very very
> Distant relative. (178)

Bourgeois death is viewed as discontinuity, a violation of the individual self which is resolvable only by the illusion of immortality.

The young, seeking escape from the suffocating life of their parents, go in search of a violent death, a death which will overcome the discontinuity of their individual selves if it is made to serve a future community. The poem focuses on the moment of recognition, in which the young discover that death is in the process of things, in the "dry-rot" of history.

The subsequent two poems instance divergent responses to this discovery. The one—employing a mockingly overrhymed, overstressed ballad stanza and an overworked economic metaphor—is turned against the bourgeois speaker whose way of life death foredooms. The other—in an irregular blank verse, with long periodic phrases—evinces the voice of one who accepts change, refusing either to deny it or to succumb to it—refusing, that is, to retreat into the old forms of explanation or, in despair, to accelerate the end. The latter voice is calm and reasoned; the former, desperate in its pacified jauntiness.

The fourth, fifth, and sixth poems move toward an "overture" for the present, in which death must be adjusted to the new metaphysic of life—the prayer for our time:

> O lord of leisure, since we know
> Your image we shall ne'er outgrow,
> Teach us the value of our stay
> Lest we insult the living clay.
>
> This clay that binds the roots of man
> And firmly foots his flying span—
> Only this clay can voice, invest,
> Measure and frame our mortal best. (182—83)

The Marxist sympathy remains, with its materialistic ground and rejection of transcendence; but it remains essentially in the humanist insistence that, even if our heart be not changed, we may learn together to care and hence not to care. Giving obedience to our mortality, we will wish no more than what we can attain within it:

> Lord of us all, now it is true
> That we are lords of all but you,
> Teach us the order of our day
> Least we deface the honoured clay. (183)

In the fifth poem the impact of Day Lewis' father's sudden death provides the instance of the passing of the old order. But that death simply extends the process of dying to its successor. Death is the continuity of generations, the universal of man. The present self, in the sixth poem, is a dying self, sentience growing inexorably dull:

> It is not you I fear, but the humiliations
> You mercifully use to deaden grief—
> The downward graph of natural joys,
> Imagination's slump, the blunted ears. (185)

The only alternative to individual death, that progressive ingrown chill, is to throw the self into history, not to deny it. Thus the poem ends with its politics married to its metaphysics and with both joined to unevasive rationalization. The workers, intimate with death, thus defy their individual mortality with unyielding persistence; it becomes so much a part of them that it has no particular identity apart from them. Death, or change, to them can only mean, to echo Hopkins, no worse, for there is none. It can only mean the evolution of things as they are, the undoing of the present state into a redeemed time:

> You were never far nor fable,
> Judgment nor happy end:
> We have come to think of you, mister, as
> Almost the family friend. (186)

Thus the answer to death is to use him—not to live against the end but to live as if it were ever present. Death becomes the will of history, the essential antithesis in the dialectic, and not as for bourgeois man, with more than his personal self at stake, a reaper of man's possessions.

Along with "The Nabara," "Overtures to Death" culminates a decade of faith for Day Lewis—a decade in which he could usually resolve his major problems, the identity of the "buried Day," by projecting it into its commitments. But paradoxically, as his commitments progressed from an emotional to an ideological base—and Day Lewis from poet to public figure—the belief in those commitments began to wane. Inevitably, his best poetry was produced out of the clash of loyalties, the counterpull of conscious and unconscious self at war in the middle of historical facts which were constantly altering the equation. There is little doubt that by 1938 events in Russia had all but destroyed the enthusiasm among the better English artists for the future Communist state. But in doing so, history made clear that the poets' flirtation with practical causes and ideological hopes was based on their enduring compassion for man and that, if their art were to survive the perturbations of history, it must not lose itself entirely in the topical and the immediate. Yet it could not live without the particular and immediate.

In the 1930's, we can safely say, the artist was not so greatly tempted to flirtation with the abstract universal, except that he desperately needed some new universal to replace those that were dying. Since the universal had to be in the material, it was a good time to return to earth, which, though it taxed flights of lyricism, provided a new human intimacy. The shifting of ground stimulated new hopes and demanded, consequently, a new poetics. But it led ironically to a retrenchment of traditional styles and modes and to a suspicion of art itself, especially of modernist experiments. It brought home to Day Lewis very clearly his true allegiances with the past and the inescapability of its fate in a world constantly changing. In this regard, the true radical poetry, like surrealism, was dismissed as escapist or condemned as antisocial, though it claimed that the true community of man was accessible only in the unconscious. But for Day Lewis, the Lawrencean unconscious was bourgeois unconscious. The poet's job was not to invent a new language but to connect the present through tradition with its origins and to make history continuous once more.

CHAPTER 5

Journey from the Frontier

IN THE tense, convulsive years of the 1930's, Day Lewis had achieved prominence as a new if not entirely original voice—the singer of a new world, of a redeemable history. It was the voice, as he would later put it, of a "future-fan"; but it also was not entirely his own voice. By the time of *Overtures to Death*, political realities like the Spanish Civil War had served to dim his faith in futures and had returned to him, from the Marxist tradition, something of his individual talent. He later termed this talent the "lyric impulse," that very energy he had lamented in *A Hope for Poetry* as the dying voice in a world that called for collective action as against individual irresponsibility. For behind "lyrical poetry we feel a certain irresponsibility."

Whatever the degree of Day Lewis' originality as a poet-of-the-1930's the voice he assumed then was, in part at least, thrust upon him by historical contingency and by social circumstance—events that threatened his innate sense of community. The dismal historical failures of ideology in the late 1930's did not exactly deprive him of his subject since he was never an ideologue at heart. It did, however, deprive him of the idea of an epiphanic future, which any new community depended upon, and it thrust him into a futureless present. In *Overtures to Death* he was forced to reconceive his future in graver, starker, less transcendental terms. In the years immediately following, he would have to find that future in his past—not simply in the tradition to which he had always sentimentally clung, but in the a priori of his unconscious where innocence, the universal, and the eternal (which is to say, the idealized and renewable past) exist and are accessible.

I   *The New Communalism*

Something like this faith in the communal self within is the burden of his series of Clark Lectures, delivered at Cambridge in 1946 and published as *The Poetic Image.*[1] His best, though in many ways his

most derivative, book of criticism, *The Poetic Image* fundamentally
sums up Day Lewis' transitions of allegiance in the immediate
post-1930's better than the poetry does. Without ideology to replace
the old, failed religion, the poet was left not only with the old need for
order or "system" but with the sole responsibility for satisfying it. He
had to return to the well of some communal unconscious; for the
fountain of history and tradition, if it had failed him, could not be
denied. And yet, this search for the "buried self," as he later called it, is
not unlike his more obvious social commitments; it is a return to the
innermost roots of the past (the collective consciousness) by way of
measuring the present and projecting a future. It is an attempt to realize
the myth of self-renewal which must exist in tension with the reality of
history. The poet whose recurrent metaphor had been the journey was
still far from the home (not to mention the magnetic mountain) he
sought. But, instead of making the journey into the mysterious future
across evanescent frontiers (poems of ideological faith which project a
space *to be* arrived at, that is, *to be* filled with life), he discovered the
satisfactions of making images (that is, poems) of that home—those
"notable images of virtue" that he more and more identified as the
resolute wholeness of art set against the chaos of life.

Two very different yet complementary events mark Day Lewis'
transition into the 1940's: the war, of course, and the disintegration of
his marriage. The war brought a quick end to the abstract subtleties of
ideological conflict and ushered in a time of moral simplicities. The
complex moral and social (even proto-religious) antinomies of capitalism and communism gave way before an even more fundamental
holy war between good and evil—the alliance of republican and
Communist states against Fascism. As Day Lewis forthrightly put it in a
little verse called "Where are the War Poets?":

> It is the logic of our times,
> No subject for immortal verse—
> That we who lived by honest dreams
> Defend the bad against the worse. (*Collected Poems,* 228)

The issues of the war were, for the most part, too clear and urgent to
stimulate a rich poetry (except where the poet's intimate involvement
with its immediate incongruities and dislocations provided occasions
and even metaphors of more than ideological relevance),[2] and its
realities were in many cases too horrible to be contemplated at a poetic
distance. And, we hasten to add, poets like Day Lewis were too morally
committed to see the war with the detachment available to a later

generation who would find the moral clarities blurring into the metaphysical absurd.

Strange though it is, Day Lewis was not a good war poet—perhaps because he had little direct experience of it (except as a member of the home guard)—but more probably because it did not provoke in him any intense personal conflict or division of loyalties, as had the challenge of Marxism to his deep emotional ties with the English past. Later, in *The Poetic Image*, he argued that the war, in contrast to the ideological conflicts of the 1930's, had rekindled the "general imagination" (108, 110); hence, it had provided the poet with an audience more receptive to the style and thought of war poetry than the public of the previous decade had been to political ideologies. Day Lewis' argument smacks of Eliot's plea for an homologous audience and a timeless language; indeed, the book concludes with a rather problematic defense of tradition which manifests its authority to the poet in the guise of communal archetypes that guarantee him certain universal themes and images and a human audience to share them. But, if the war rekindled the "general imagination," it did not rekindle Day Lewis', nor did it move him to respond strikingly to its "common experience."

His war poems are largely conventional pieces—filled with anger; with compassion for the innocent victim, the wounded and the dying; and with solemn awe for the common sacrifices. These poems occupy but a modest amount of his consciousness. The war, like the collapse of his marriage, comes to be a metaphor for a greater theme: the inevitable breakup of the old order; the death that follows change and precedes rebirth; the inevitable violence of change (and history) that is paradoxically its essence. Like love, war is a fit of passion, an outburst of that creative-destructive energy from which life springs and by which life is victimized. Day Lewis did not callously or indifferently turn war into metaphorical grist; it only confirmed his discovery that in poetry alone, poetry which transforms experience into universally valid metaphors, could history be contained and rendered morally coherent.

The breakup of his marriage, which of course was more personally traumatic, resulted in a number of imaginative attempts to catch its reality and its meaning. In the pain of that slowly disintegrating relationship, Day Lewis sought an answer for his own inability to control events he was intimately involved in; he sought some "knowledge" of human necessity. Violence and the beautiful terror of passion, the instability of human relationships, the ceaselessly changing nature of the self, the need for love as a binding constant for community—these were themes not altogether different from those of the 1930's, except that any intellectual structure for containing them had failed and their true "romantic" origin had become clearer. Those earlier intellectual structures (the "tetragonal/ Pure symmetry of brain" in *Transitional Poem*, or the variations on Marxism that turned into a communal myth) were, as Day Lewis states in *Poetic Image*, his variants on the "great educative myths which from the earliest times inch by inch enticed man forward out of his brutishness . . . making amenable the recalcitrant earth and the dangerous spirits by mastering them in imagination, promoting religion to control superstition" (32). In this same paragraph, on the role of myth in the evolution of mind, Day Lewis remarks that the old myths "are dead" ". . . because, having performed their evolutionary task, they were needed no more. Emerging from the collective mind and illuminating it during the centuries when there was no other light, their task nevertheless was to set man on his own feet, teach him to walk by himself, to think and feel for himself, no longer one unit in a living aggregate but an individual human being. So the poetic myths are dead: and the poetic image, which is the myth of the individual, reigns in their stead" (32). Day Lewis treats myth, like the modern anthropologist, as a mode of interpretation—as man's attempt at a totalization of his understanding of his world.

The parallels with Eliot's traditionalism and his appeal to the "mythical method" are obvious, except that Day Lewis falls back upon the "myth of the individual" and not upon that of an institutionalized human condition. "The poetic myth," he argues in *Poetic Image*, "was created by a collective consciousness; the poetic image returns to that consciousness for its sanction. It is not merely that, time and again, we find in the images of modern poetry forms and impulses derived from the myths; but the very nature of the image—of poetry in its metaphorical aspect—invokes that consciousness, as though man, even at his most individual, still seeks emotional reassurance from the sense of community, not community with his fellow-beings alone, but with whatever is living in the universe, and with the dead" (32–33). Thus Day Lewis rationalized what we may call a shift from the objective to the subjective ground of community.

As Spender had argued at the close of the 1930's, the poet needs an orthodoxy in which to contain the chaos of modernity, but "political orthodoxy has a great disadvantage: it leaves nothing to the imagination," while religious orthodoxy is "a structure within which great art can exist, because however strictly it may be defined, the main terms are mysterious and leave room for invention and contemplation."[3]

For all too brief a time political orthodoxy of one kind had seemed to Day Lewis and even to Spender to provide the essential latitude of mystery; certainly, we must observe that the concern over the failure of ideology as religion was both common and urgent in the late 1930's. And, though Day Lewis was hesitant about the possibilities of a new religious orthodoxy, his "myth of the individual," the belief in the "poetic image," was what he had instead of God. It is, as it were, a belief in the poet and his commitment, and in the act of imagination by which he comes to know his emerging self. The poetic image is the structure of some primordial event, of the mystery of origins, and whether the poet consciously alludes to mythology or linguistically structures his private experience, he is participating in the "community" of the "poetic image."

II *Love and War*

In 1940 Day Lewis published a modest sheaf of verse entitled *Poems in Wartime*, which three years later was incorporated into the more substantial *Word Over All*, a volume which more than anything else reveals the degree to which personal and historical pressure short-circuited his creativity. Relatively few in number, the poems are not especially distinguished, except, as John Wain has recently said, that they are more his own, less dependent on models than any he wrote before or after.[4] The war poems, referred to earlier, constitute substantially the second part of the book's three divisions and, except for the title poem, speak quietly and conventionally of compassion and pity. They are, as Clifford Dyment has said, poems which identify Day Lewis once more with his countrymen and their cause in a pact of love.[5] And that identification in itself bespeaks their lack of vitality. It is one thing to be imaginatively engaged and quite another to give the self passively and anonymously to the larger community—and a great number of the war poems assume that anonymous voice of a country wounded but self-secure in its commitment. If in the 1930's Day Lewis had found himself vitally challenged by a disintegrating world, in the landscape of war he had found community, brotherhood, love, and a role beyond alienation.

But the distinctive tone of the volume relates it to the poems of nature and childhood which stood out so purely in *Overtures to Death*. In the face of historical crisis, Day Lewis found his subject matter to be the buried self. "What links the real to the wraith?" he asked in a somewhat later poem in *Collected Poems* (248). If any motif binds together the poetry written between 1938 and 1947 it is the problematic of identity. *Word Over All* borrows its title from Whitman, though not even the title poem is Whit manesque. The "word" Day Lewis beseeches is not exactly Whitman's transcendental energy which marries life and death, purifying "this soiled world"; it is the poet's "image" which, as a poem with that title (226) puts it, is Perseus' shield to the Medusa of the present (see also *Poetic Image*, 99 and 104, for a discussion of this "image"). In this dark and guilty world of violence, death alone absolves all contradictions and assures the continuity of selves. Whitman's word was death (the immanence of unity), but Day Lewis' is love. The title poem puts his hope for poetry directly: "Words are to set man's joy and suffering there/ In constellations" (222). The contradiction in Day Lewis' art lies between his demands, on the one hand, for a self-transcending poetry, which with Whitman's energy might transmute the ordinary into the prophetic, and his inability, on the other, to escape the limits of his essential materialism. What Day Lewis lacked, in other words, was a Whitman-like faith in the transcendental origins of poetic energy and hence in a monistic world, though the essential presumption of *The Poetic Image* is the poet's faith in the immanent human order of consciousness.

Love as the binding force, then, is Day Lewis' equivalent for the "word over all." This mystique of love leads him in time of crisis back to his countrymen and provokes such sentimental occasional poems as "Watching Post" (226) and "The Stand-To" (227), which pay homage to the home-guard company he served as leader. These poems celebrate his identification with the English yeomanry, which had been evident in his early poetry and even latent in his Marxism. If love, and not sentiment, is the motivation of these poems, they are consistent with his celebrations of love's restorative power, and with his fundamental sense of love as the spiritual equivalent of science's laws of universal harmony and thus the innate source of man's need of community.

But even love, Day Lewis has to conclude in one of the volume's better poems, "The Assertion," is a force both creative and destructive. The poem opens with an irregular stanza of violent metaphors ("the fighter spinning like vertigo/ On the axis of the trapped pilot . . . "), which rhetorically concludes that in this time, "when man seems born to hurt," it is "time we assert/ To their face that men are love" (225). The urgency of assertion—the rhetorical necessity of the poem to "assert"—reflects Day Lewis' style of the 1930's rather more than the lyric style he was critically opting for. The poem ends:

> For love's no laughing matter,
> Never was a free gift, an angel, a fixed equator.
> Love's the big boss at whose side for ever slouches
> The shadow of the gunman: he's mortar and dynamite;
> Antelope, drinking pool, but the tiger too that crouches.
> Therefore be wise in the dark hour to admit
> The logic of the gunman's trigger,
> Embrace the explosive element, learn the need
> Of tiger for antelope and antelope for tiger.

Love is energy, both generative and destructive, both synthesizing yet atomizing. It is the essential emotional vitality of life and, ambiguously, the energy or force in which death lives. It is animal, both antelope and tiger, or grace and violence, fused into one—form and content.

The war poems are placed between two groups of more personally centered lyrics in the structure of *Word Over All*. The book opens with the sonnet "The Lighted House" (211) which exploits a Poesque metaphor of inner space. It is a poem of the divided self or the alienated imagination, the recluse of the house and the "dead beat traveller out of the storm" seeking a way back to refuge. His return, "Peeling off fear after fear, revealing love's true form," is in itself a metaphor of Day Lewis' own quest to make himself whole again, to marry once more unconscious and conscious, emotion and rational, timeless and historical self.

The more engaging poems of the book center upon memories, or return to the subterranean darkness of the earlier self. These poems manifest several kinds of release: most obviously, from the immediate pressures of the war. But by that very release they introduce a new conflict. Too many of them are simply nostalgic and sentimental. A few, like "Departure in the Dark" and "O Dreams, O Destinations," evince not only the old technical skill but the power of Day Lewis' submerged memories. The motif of the former derived from the poet's childhood and provided the tensions for his pervasive journey metaphor. "Nothing so sharply reminds a man he is mortal/ As leaving a place" (213), it begins; and it continues by exploring the paradox in terms of the Israelite journey from bondage into the mystery of freedom: "The desire/ Going forth meets the desire returning." The dominant mood is death, "the last of his dark departures" which, like the Israelite "desert of freedom," both attracts and repels. The poem is a personal reprise on his more ideological journeys.

The particular quality of Day Lewis' treatment of this all-too-familiar theme of desire and death lies in his ability to translate it into his own dilemma, caught as he is in the middle of his own journey in a time of violence and disintegrating personal relationships. The sonnet sequence "O Dreams, O Destinations" (216) is his most successful realization and resolution of the paradox. Its nine poems move from the child's "time" (figured in the self-contained image of a "humming shell") through his fall into time ("the ruination of innocence") and the desire to "build a road" back out of time (to restore "the appetite for wholeness" now lost), which is really an "illusion" that sustains the search. The poem, in brief, is a carefully examined look at the paradoxical desire "To escape time, always to start anew."

The success of "O Dreams, O Destinations" lies in its careful modulation of imagery, of which the first sonnet is a good example:

> For infants time is like a humming shell
> Heard between sleep and sleep, wherein the shores
> Foam-fringed, wind-fluted of the strange earth dwell
> And the sea's cavernous hunger faintly roars.
> It is the humming pole of summer lanes
> Whose sound quivers like heat-haze endlessly
> Over the corn, over the poppied plains—
> An emanation from the earth or sky.
> Faintly they hear, through the womb's lingering haze,
> A rumour of that sea to which they are born:
> They hear the ringing pole of summer days,
> But need not know what hungers for the corn.
> They are the lisping rushes in a stream—
> Grace-notes of a profound, legato dream.

The "humming shell" is a precise image of time as space, self-contained yet indefinite. It provides the basic image patterns of sea and sound, the harmonies of a totally self-sufficient realm. The "shell" is like a "womb," or the latent memory of the womb, another sea with sound, its echoes sensuous and imprecise like remembered summers. In all, this encapsulated time is a whole world, sensuous and fertile, but impalpable like a "heat-haze." The residual world of primordial memory, it is, as the second sonnet echoes, a "Tissue of mist." The "time" of the "shell" is the synchronic time of myth, poetry, dreams, and thus the "poetic image."

The shift from "shell" to clearing "mist," from a world of fertile harmonies and faintly ominous sounds to a world of emerging consciousness, delicately extends the paradox. The poet's controlling voice only recalls the child's innocence, even as it recognizes the child's compulsion to assume the world and time—that is, to fall and claim his own life. "Reaching towards the far thing, we begin it" is the theme of the third sonnet and of the poem as a whole. The fall is sensuous, sexual, theological, philosophical—experience emerging into self-consciousness, to be contained in paradoxes of form:

> Man only casts the image of his joys
> Beyond his senses' reach; and by this fateful
> Act, he confirms the ambiguous power of choice.
> Innocence made that first choice. It is she
> Who weeps, a child chained to the outraged tree. (217)

The remaining six sonnets explore the resolutions possible to one who knows he fights a war which "has no end" and whose "appetite for wholeness" is at once life will and death wish. They celebrate youth, "dead youth," as energy, the *élan vital*, youth as the "sacred river" of the self which is to be recovered, if at all, only in "illusion." The sequence as a whole forfeits the comfort of this "illusion" even while borrowing its sustenance. The poet lives on his desire for a phoenix rebirth—"To escape time, always to start anew"—but he counters wish with reality: "Travellers, we're fabric of the road we go;/ We settle, but like feathers on time's flow."

Word Over All makes it sadly evident that the times provided Day Lewis with little of the confidence necessary for either sustaining illusion or confronting reality. He did not find the encompassing "Word," and he seldom generated the shielding "image" of a pure poetry. That is, he did not have the time to find his own voice, though almost every poem evinces his recognition that he must find it and that it resides in some arcane realm of an earlier self:

> What links the real to the wraith?
> My self repudiates myself of yesterday;
> But the words it lived in and cast like a shell keep faith
> With that dead self always. (248)

Living in time and change, the poet's very act (manifest in language) lives on the death of his earlier self. Language is continuous with the past and his earlier self, and in it he fulfills his commerce with the past and things eternal, the center of a purer imagination. The act of poetry remained a two-way journey, away from the earlier self yet toward it. Like the seashell, the poem builds layers of time upon itself, discovering the continuity within history's apparent discontinuities.

III *Modern Love*

Poems 1943–1947 is a more coherent and satisfactory book, if only because it is obsessed with the meaning and consequences of one primary event: the breakup of his marriage, or, as he put it in the opening poem, "The Double Vision" (*Collected Poems*, 247): "how most human loves protract/ Themselves to unreality—the fact/ Drained of its virtue by the image it made." The poem serves as prologue to Day Lewis' own *Modern Love*. For obvious reasons, George Meredith is the governing spirit of the book; and in 1948, when Day Lewis contributed an introduction to a new edition of *Modern Love*, he interpreted Meredith's achievement as a foreshadowing of his own time, when a rigid but not necessarily virtuous system of ethics (Victorian morality) fell away, throwing the ethical center back upon the finite self: "Strength of feeling is made the supreme sanction for a state of affairs it has already caused, and by which it is therefore compromised: the warring mind becomes sole judge over the conflict that divides it: the victim is required to be also his own inquisitor, adviser and support."[6] Day Lewis' admiration for Meredith is not fully explained by their similar marital situations. What he sought in Meredith was a kindred spirit, one who like himself stood at a historical and moral watershed where the old sense of metaphysical and social community was giving way to a post-Romantic sense of individual isolation in a centerless universe. Thomas Hardy shares with Meredith this role of spiritual ancestor; and associated with them is Emily Brontë, who inspires one poem and later was the subject of one of Day Lewis' more penetrating essays.[7] For Miss Brontë is Day Lewis' figure of the "beating wings" of desire in a purely dehumanized cosmos. The creative passion incarnate, she is "Chained to a dream" and "Burning for pure freedom" (279); but she lived nonetheless with the conscious knowledge of necessity. Similarly Hardy, who confronted the same despair not with "beating wings" of passionate revolt but with a mordant irony that modulated hate into compassion, helplessness into stoicism.

This retreat to an earlier generation, predecessors of the Georgians whose willed innocence had so affected Day Lewis as a child and alienated him as a young man, has perplexed a number of critics who regard it as another form of turning away from the present. Anthony Thwaite, for example, has puzzled over how one judges a "20th century poet who, after helping achieve the poetic revolution of our time, reacts in his prime by writing work which is pastiche—very competent pastiche—of two eminent Victorian critics (Meredith and Hardy)."[8] Perhaps because Thwaite ascribes more originality to Day Lewis' "poetic revolution" than it deserves, he fails to see that the poet's turning to appropriate predecessors is consistent with his traditionalism

and even with his Marxism. Moreover, the retreat is consistent with his
understanding that, when the system fails, then the center of authority
is returned to the Romantic self. Yet this mortal self is neither stable
nor enduring; it is "divided."

The coherence of self, Day Lewis had always concluded, depends on
the coherence of the culture (the system) which subsumes it—thus his
stress on family; his sense of divorce as the living present. His argument
for the primacy of environment went back at least to the Preface of
Oxford Poetry, 1927. Seeking identification with earlier poets who
were confronted by the same dilemma of a disintegrating system, Day
Lewis was in effect seeking the only community and tradition
remaining to him—the creative mind whose passionate longing for
freedom and order was in itself the only freedom and order. In short,
Day Lewis' retreat is another affirmation of the mind which manifests
its wholeness in the "poetic image." If his poets are not exactly
legislators to man, they are at least passionate opponents of man's (and
history's) chaos.

The larger part of the *Poems 1943–1947* consists of a Meredithian
sequence on the growth, flowering, and failure of human love; or, in
Day Lewis' somewhat expanded variation, it is an autobiographical
sequence which occasionally imitates Meredith by slipping into a
psychological mode, assuming the point of view of the woman, and
playing out the ironies of a dialogue in which there is no communication. But, above and beyond the obviously personal instigation, the
sequence is devoted first to a search for the earlier self (the "wraith" to
his present "real" self), and second to what Day Lewis called, when
speaking of *Modern Love*, the "moral, psychological and poetic truth"
of man's victimization by his passions: "We are betrayed by what is
false within."[9] The two themes are complementary. The craving for
what Meredith called the "buried day" (the phrase Day Lewis borrowed
for the title of his memoirs) he saw to be the nostalgia for some past
ideal relationship, the analogue of primal unity, and hence a wish (a
kind of death wish?) that human relationships might be finally stable.

The enduring modern quality of Meredith's sequence, as Day Lewis
saw it, was that it gave the moral, psychological, and poetic lie to this
nostalgic idyl. Day Lewis' own excavations of memory are testimony to
his belief that poetry is not the lesson but the experience of truth;
hence, he must peel away the layers of his relationships back to the
moment of innocence that apparently preceded them, thus disabusing
himself of the idea that he could ever relive the past. For only by
escaping nostalgia could he relive the past: be reborn in a new and fresh

love, not chained to the ambiguities of a nostalgic one or the regretful memory of one that has failed.

The autobiographical sequence in *Poems 1943–1947* opens with a prologue ("The Double Vision"); plunges into the remembered earlier self ("Juvenilia" and "Sketches for a Self-Portrait") in an attempt to find the seeds of his deficiency in later relationships; then develops through four Meredithian variations on the marriage relationship ("Marriage of Two," "Married Dialogue," "The Woman Alone," and "Ending"); and concludes with two speculations on the meaning of love's failure ("Heart and Mind" and "A Failure"). Needless to say, Day Lewis does not presume to do anything so daring or sustained as *Modern Love*. And it is revealing that he is most different from Meredith in the degree to which he is obsessed with his earlier, youthful self as being unprepared for enduring relationships.

"Juvenilia" (247) and "Sketches for a Self-Portrait" (250) are the two most successful poems in the sequences. The former is a tightly composed exploration of the "primitive mural" of an earlier self, upon which the present self is "superimposed." In this poem of time, the bewildered self which thinks of itself as organically continuous discovers that the present self lives in the successive deaths of the earlier. The relationship of the "real to the wraith" perplexes and casts light on the present death of love which he is suffering:

> And since at every stage I need
> A death, a new self to reveal me,
> And only through oblivion's veil can read
> The signs of what befell me,
> May not the grave of rigored love
> Be but one more abyss
> Between two peaks, appointed to compel me
> Along the chain of light? (249)

Whether the poem will bear the weight of its sexual puns (on death) is a question made irrelevant only because of its imprecise appeal to the sentimental vision of rebirth.

"Sketches," which is less successful as a total poem, is more abundant in snippets, actual and emblematic, of Day Lewis' formative years. It is a poem of the fall from innocence—a poem of solitude and longing, or, in a striking metaphor, his "*coitus interruptus* with a cheating world" (251). Most revealing is his struggle to contain the world in words, the urgency of the self-conscious self to recover his oneness with the world in language:

> Oh, innocent vice—
> Could everything be reduced to a form of words!
> But they were only a guesswork map of the terrain
> Where soon I should have to fight; or else a petition
> To be exempted. (253)

Like so many others in this time-obsessed book, the poem is structured upon the paradox of the poet's (child's and lover's) desire to compose his own world within world, to contain reality in words, to annex the other, all the while aware that the struggle little avails. The primordial language is contained within the words he speaks but is no longer available in its purity. The actuality of the marriage destroys the illusion of a stable world, either a self-centered world of words or one built on enduring relationships. The present relationship embodies "a thousand repetitions/ Of a routine immemorial" (254). The failure of love becomes the metaphysical norm of present history. "Marriage of Two" (254) and "Married Dialogue" (255) move sharply from paradox to irony; and "The Woman Alone" (258) strives, after Meredith, to project into the female conscience by way of catching the ultimate and inevitable failure of love—built ironically on a passion which exists only to destroy itself. For passion is the complement and antithesis of the creative imagination. The metaphorical male-female antithesis and dialectic of his earlier poetry comes into focus in the actuality of his lived experience only to become metaphor once more.

Poems 1943–1947 is intrinsically time-haunted, whether Day Lewis is exploring the instability of love or the essential life of "images." "New Year's Eve" (272), the only moderately long piece in the book, reveals the essential preoccupations. Without Audenesque contortions, challenging even the clichéd motif of the year's simultaneous death and rebirth, the poem seems to resolve for Day Lewis the ambiguities of lived time ("Walled up in time"), the phoenix life of passion, love, and human relations of all kinds: "Bound by the curse of man—/ To live in his future, which is to live surely/ In his own death—we endure the embrace of the present/ But yearn for a being beyond us" (274). The poem is in two parts: an Ode, which examines the paradox of living in time (that is, in consciousness) which drives man to live "in his future"; and a Meditation, which offers the only resolution to living one's own death, in either past or future. The solution is to live fully in the present, that eternally transitional ground between the two. For the present is "nothing unless it is spun from/ A live thread out of the past"; and the poet can only conclude:

> To live the present, then, not to live for it—
> Let this be one of today's
> Resolutions; and the other, its corollary,
> To court the commonplace. (277)

Day Lewis' need to "look with the naked eye of the Now" and hence "to witness the rare in the common" is in effect the need of the poet to live in his act of poetry. This need is derived from his fall into a world without magic, unless in his own powers he can find the eloquence of the ordinary. In other words, to live the present—the present informed by the tinges of memory—is to live in the moment of creating the poem, objectifying the self in the world, and hence to live in the constant remaking of the self: "My flesh and blood, themselves a web of experience discarded, renewed, amassed" (277). "New Year's Eve" is in effect Day Lewis' final repudiation of the Marxist apocalypse, which after all had always been a dubious consolation. His materialism in the 1930's had rejected the more idealistic qualities of Marxism for its more pragmatic and immediate virtue of action. In short, as he came to distrust the past which latently held him, he could not wholly leap into the compelling future: he had to find some way of living the "Now," that moment of transition, like New Year's Day, between past and future. Only in the act of poetry could it be both lived and conserved.

It is not surprising that Day Lewis found not only Hardy and Meredith but Paul Valéry his poet of the moment. And, while Day Lewis' translation of "La Cimetière de marin" into a rather literal English meditative poem indicated an unwillingness or inability to follow Valéry into the absolute abstraction of a purely poetic (and for Valéry, purely mental) world, the act of translation testifies to Day Lewis' interest in at least one aspect of Valéry's theory and practice: his stress on the self-creative (or self-re-creating) act of mind—the poem as purification and renewal. For Day Lewis, however, renewal did not necessarily mean purification in the sense Valéry implies. For Day Lewis, it seems to suggest only that rebirth of the stagnant social self: the act by which, reembracing the present with its incessant change, one survived the inevitable death of one's own passion and the love it recurrently creates and destroys: " . . . though my days are/ Repetitive, dull, disjointed," he writes, "I must continue to practice them over and over/ Like a five-finger exercise" (278). Poetry ritualizes time and lends to one's days whatever sanctity they may have.

In the early 1950's, shortly after his second marriage, Day Lewis undertook a long, unorthodox "travel" poem in which, as in *Tran-*

sitional Poem, he attempted to reassess the potential wholeness of the self. But he was by this time no longer convinced, as he had earlier been, of the "tetragonal/ Pure symmetry of brain." On the contrary, the totality of self could no longer be contemplated in the image of a composed space; it had to be seen as stretched upon the time of its consciousness (the duration of the past or memory, present or sensation, and future or idea). This shift from a view of self as *essence* to a view of self as *being* is integral to Day Lewis' changing style, a preparation for the more modestly humanist poetry of the last two decades: the "permanent myth," as he called it in *Poetic Image*, of man's "unending struggle with his fate" (157).

IV *The Longest Journey*

An Italian Visit, Day Lewis' longest single poem, is another transitional piece. Published in 1953 as a single volume, it serves not only to introduce a third phase of his poetic career but to compose those fragmentary, fugitive explorations of the divided self which preoccupied him in the 1940's. Taking his epigraph from Jasper More's *The Land of Italy*, Day Lewis returned to his journey metaphor, this time to snatch the putative fulfillment denied him in earlier years: "an Italian visit is a voyage of discovery," More wrote, "not only of scenery and cities, but also of the latent faculties of the traveller's heart and mind" (*Collected Poems*, 303). This poem concerns the tripartite self recomposed, made whole in self-knowledge, or in the consciousness of its various nature made whole, that is, in the language of the poem, man's only possible "ideal home" (356).

An Italian Visit returned momentarily to the ambitious and contrived poems of Day Lewis' earlier invention and turned away from the lyrical mode toward which his style had been developing. In this sense, the poem of intellectual accounting is self-consciously transitional, the kind of poem he seemed compelled to write at given intervals. As such, it returned to Day Lewis' earlier analytic mode, treating the self as a composite of abstractions, as the meeting point of three degrees of time consciousness. Yet despite its strategy, the poem is an attempt to move beyond this simplified view of self, to catch (in the image of a continuous dialogue) the interacting consciousness of historical man who is struggling to satisfy his appetite to live simultaneously in a world composed of immediate sensation, memory, and the a priori of received ideas or given language.

Day Lewis' strategy is to use a kind of populist persona and to effect a kind of dramatic narrative. (The poem is, of course, a metaphorical condensation of his own trip to Italy after his second marriage.) The single self (or traveler) of the poem is three: Tom, Dick, and Harry, who represent, respectively, the hedonist, the traditionalist, and the idealist. To see them another way, Tom lives for the moment, the life of sensation, the present; Dick sees the present only in terms of the past, his imagination determined by the authority of tradition; and Harry is both analytic and synthetic, concerned with past and present only as evidence from which to project the possible, the future. The end of the poem is predictable within this beginning, and it suffers from contrivance. But the work is Day Lewis' last attempt at a major poem, which is to say, a major self-integration. For if an Italian journey is a voyage of discovery and an initiation rite, it is also, as every Englishman knows, a health cure—a new beginning.

Divided into seven parts, *An Italian Visit* affects a variety of styles, each limited by the demands of a somewhat colloquial dialogue, the conventions of descriptive poetry, and deliberate parody. Because the poem tends to be what one reviewer called reportage,[10] the style dissipates both its intellectual and emotional effect. The sacrifice, we suspect, is something Day Lewis willingly made in order to reach a wider audience with what might otherwise be an unpopular intellectual poem. In this sense, it would be but another of his periodic attempts to reduce the distance between poet and audience. Interestingly and revealingly, the poem reaches out, on the one hand, to the common reader and, on the other, to the poetic tradition—an attempt to take the measure, we presume, of the poet that Day Lewis had discovered himself to be.

An Italian Visit opens with a "Dialogue at the Airport" which establishes the points of view of Tom, Dick, and Harry. Their fixed consciousnesses, ironically, are not changed by the visit but rather are confirmed by it, and, in that moment of recognition, reunified. The change is in the total self, the harmonizing of the self's diverse and conflicting allegiances in the awareness that each in and by itself is incomplete. Their first destination is Rome, the Eternal City, the manifest Past; and their anticipations of Rome define each. Only Dick views the city as the "nonpareil," away from which all history has led and to which all values must return. For Tom history is irrelevant: the old world provides only new sensations which set in motion the "primitive dance" of the senses. And Harry considers the journey as a means, and hence the necessary incidental, to a greater end:

> Yes, travel is travail: a witless
> Ordeal of self-abasement to an irreversible process.
> It would be nice, waking as it were from twilight, sleep, to
> Find the new bourne beside one. (309)

Harry knows the meaning of journeys—"Each journey's a bid for the empyrean/ Of absolute freedom" (311)—but his living for the future is, as Day Lewis puts it in "New Year's Eve," "to live surely/ In [one's] own death" (279). The dialogue at the airport is a tangle of partial perspectives, any one of which cannot exist without the other: Tom's *tabula rasa* of the senses (or in another image, his pure film) can record no distinct pattern without Dick's a priori forms, or the enduring image of tradition which conveys value and order into the present. And, without either the vital "now" or the anterior order, Harry has no foundation to project from fact to idea, from experience to truth. Harry is an Audenesque consciousness, the follower of Groddeck, Freud, and Marx; and a futurist who would dismiss the past were it not that reality, after all, was idea—some eternally repeated pattern like the dance. Harry represents the rationalist mind in which Day Lewis placed so much trust in *Transitional Poem*, and in Harry's perspective the partial wisdoms of Tom and Dick are completed. Once the points of view are established, Day Lewis repeats the ideas to excess, lest they be confused. And, in a rhetorical style that is neither distinguished dialogue nor intellectually concise, he betrays his dual purpose to write an intellectual poem for the common audience.

In the second section of *An Italian Visit*, however, Day Lewis modulates his style into a descriptive-narrative sequence. The stylistic changes in the volume recall, in fact, the structural variation of *A Time to Dance*. Part Two, "Flight to Italy," is nevertheless an indulgence, a playing with extravagant metaphors. The airplane is conceived in the hyperbolic image of a "bull": the flight as Europa's journey to Crete. Moreover, the plane is a "womb," the journey (like that of the fetus in *From Feathers to Iron*) a "trance prenatal." In short, the flight is a journey of renewal; the arrival at Rome, a "phoenix moment." The description of the flight, however, resists the metaphorical weight thrust upon it; for Day Lewis' insistence on the mythical relevance of the flight is lost in the imagistic detail of modern technology. The total effect recalls Day Lewis poetry of the 1930's—a verse that renders occasionally striking images and metaphors but, on the whole, loses intensity by not synthesizing its parts.

Part Three shifts once more, to the Audenesque "letter" form.

Called "A Letter from Rome," it is a disquisition on ideological naivete, and most particularly on the failure of Day Lewis' generation to take proper cognizance of the past and tradition. It is a confessional poem above all:

> We who "flowered" in the Thirties
> Were an odd lot; sceptical yet susceptible,
> Dour though enthusiastic, horizon-addicts
> And future-fans, terribly apt to ask what
> Our all-very-fine sensations were in aid of.
> We did not, you will remember, come to coo.
> Still, there is hope for us. Rome has absorbed
> Other barbarians: yes, and there's nobody quite so
> Sensuously rich and reckless as the reformed
> Puritan. . . . This by the way, to establish a viewpoint. (322)

The viewpoint of "A Letter from Rome" is that of an "horizon addict" who has lost his faith in futures, whose time is running out, and who desperately needs to set present history in past perspective if he is to know any possible future. Rome, the manifest record of history's "grand design," is marked here and there by the present and its "abject means." Rome is the accumulation of myths, and hence of human meanings—of those forms which, the more they change, the more they remain the same. Hence Rome is "eternal," yet present: " . . . but a sense of the past, to be truly/Felicitous, demands some belief in the present. . . . " Buried in Rome, now a part of that past yet symbols of alienation from their and the poet's tradition, are Keats and Shelley. And, as the poet stands by their graves, he hears the incongruous blare of jazz "drowned by the ghost of a nightingale." But, amid this "family of exiles," the poet finds himself and discovers his inevitable role. He thus feels at home, yet he turns away once more to move on to Florence, the cradle of the Renaissance and the last great period of a transcendental art.

"Bus to Florence," Part Four, is an eloquent, largely descriptive travelogue that serves more to alter the scene of the poem than to advance its theme. Yet it serves a rather subtle function in the larger sequence. A poem of love, it is dedicated to the poet's "beautiful creature" (his new wife?), who has reintegrated his sensibility. The recording of impressions of the journey evinces this new sensitiveness, this renewal. The journey itself through the ancient Italian countryside is a return, as it were, to a "simple time," a magical time, a time preceding Rome's awesome formalizations of belief—but it is a world into which the modern consciousness can only "dip." "It's sequence I lack, the talent to grasp/ Not a here-and-there phrase/ But the music entire, its original strain and logic" (332), the poet recognizes. What he lacks, in other words, is what love in part restores: the emotional cohesion to his fragmentary intellect. At the end of the ride, he and his bride alight as one; he is renewed and made whole in her presence; she has become his "eyes."

And Part Five moves on to what her eyes (the synthetic feminine vision) see. Called "Florence: Works of Art," it is the most ambitious piece in the sequence, a complex look at man's struggle to know the "all-encroaching" Past by way of knowing himself. The section begins with a formal address to Florence as the unavailable Past, whose glory is "catalogued,/ A norm for scholars and for gentlemen":

> Plodding the galleries, we ask how can
> That century of the Uncommon Man,
> Sovereign here in paint, bronze, marble, suit
> The new narcissism of the Also-Ran.

The poet-tourist hopes not to recapture the Past but to be elevated by it; not to repeat his heritage but to fulfill it. But he lives in the pedestrian century of the common man, a centerless, solipsistic time.

The greater part of the fifth section consists of five parodies, each a poem based on a piece of classical Renaissance art, the style of each poem a parody of a by-now classical modern poet: Luca Della Robbia's *Singing Children* as interpreted by Hardy; Donatello's *Judith and Holofernes*, by Yeats; Leonardo's *Annunciation*, by Frost; Piero di Cosimo's *Perseus Rescuing Andromeda*, by Auden; and Verrochio's *Boy with Dolphin*, by Dylan Thomas. Though of varying quality and aptness, the parodies are consistently clever if not always penetrating. Those "by" Frost and Auden are especially sensitive to stylistic nuance, the Auden poem being cast in Auden's own ironic stanza form of "Under Which Lyre," a poem mocking the age of the common man. The Yeats poem parodies "A Prayer for My Daughter," while the Hardy and Thomas pieces essentially echo the gestures of ironist and apocalyptic, respectively.

But the strategy of the parodies is central to the poem's theme. The five Renaissance masters which serve as inspiration submit only reluctantly to the modern styles. And, in turn, the five moderns are frustrated in their efforts to penetrate the intrinsic order of the earlier culture. The parodies, in other words, present the dilemma of the modern who must create order, not reflect that of a coherent past he feels to be a part of his being. The style of the modern is his own atom of meaning, distinct from every other. The Renaissance masters uncommonly reflect a common and coherent world; the five poets translate Renaissance *concordia discors* into modern alienation, the modern myth, the "myth of the individual" as Day Lewis' called in the *The Poetic Image*. And Day Lewis, in his own parodic alliance with his modern masters and peers, realizes the tentativeness of his ties with tradition, the blurred effort. The confession of his tendency to imitate becomes an explanation of it:

> And if I miss that radiance where it flies,
> Something is gained in the mere exercise
> Of strenuous submission, the attempt
> To lose and find oneself through others' eyes. (339)

The last two parts of *An Italian Visit* are the least successful of the group. Part Six, "Elegy Before Death: At Settignano," is a series of reflections on time: on how to capture in a "melting Now the formula/ Of always" (345). It is, in brief, a poem of resignation, an embrace of time and the Paradise of the Now in which man has only brief "tenure." The lesson of Florence and Rome has been the lesson of history as change, of the eternal as change. Thus the concluding section, cast in the form of a "Homeward Prospect," returns to Tom, Dick, and Harry once more for their respective gleanings from the journey. Tom is full of new sensations; Dick, grown dour that the Past he has touched cannot be repossessed; Harry, now somewhat distrustful of the "elegant systems" into which he has cast experience and projected a future.

The return home is toward a new kind of wholeness. The journey into the Past has made contact with the unconscious and memory—not alone the personal but the cultural consciousness. But the retreat, as Day Lewis views it, is not like Eliot's historical nostalgia. It is an understanding of history as myth, the accumulation of man-centered forms. Just as the Dick of every self must be complemented by the Tom, the teleology of any Harry must be projected cautiously from the substance of new sensations and from the knowledge of memory. Environment (if no longer brute materialism) continues its hold on Day Lewis, heavily qualifying his faith in the "tetragonal/ Pure symmetry of brain."

The poem ends with a series of speculations on "home." To Harry, home is the place where we "inter our travels" (empirical experiences) so that they might "germinate" into ideas which protect us, like dreams, against the brute fact of routine or time. For Tom, home is a place of continually new sensations. And for Dick, it is the place one "can never quit": "An ideal home, if you like, which you spend a lifetime building/ Out of whatever comes to hand" (356). Home, to put it simply, is the composed world of the poem, the ideal wholeness of the "poetic image" toward which each poetic journey—even though leading away into the Past—moves. It is a "home," however, built of fragments out of the means at hand. The modern poet does not take his inspiration from God, but is what the French anthropologist Claude Lévi-Strauss calls a *bricoleur* or craftsman who builds with whatever means are available rather than having his materials cut to a predesigned plan. Metaphysically, the difference between the *bricoleur* and the engineer, the man who must improvise and the man who constructs by design, is the difference between a world with a center (God or logos) and a world without a center. In Day Lewis' world, the only center is self-divided man, who must pull the Tom, Dick, and Harry of himself together again. Home, thus, is the place where experience germinates into reality, where idea and act coexist. It is an ideal of self, with its divided parts recomposed. But, if it is the ideal image of a completed poem, so is it the ideal end of a fully realized self—like the tombs of Keats and Shelly.

An Italian Visit, strange as it may seem, is a poem about the poetic process and, hence, about the life process: based on the faith of renewal, and on the dream that man sustains himself in his struggle to become whole again, even if his wholeness lies only at the end of all journeys, the "empyrean future" that is death. If, in the end, the poet recognizes this dream of wholeness is illusion, the illusion is nonetheless an animus. The struggle does avail; the poet lives in building his home, in renewing himself. The journey is inward and backward, but only to return to the now, not to escape time. Its destination is the mystery of the human, which alone dreams beyond itself in order to live in the now. In that dream, it learns to live in its own death: "Losing my heart to this alien land, I renew my true love:/ Lending my love to death, I gained this grain of vision./ I took my pen. What I wrote is thanks to her and to Italy" (148). These are the poem's closing lines and also the last ones of Day Lewis' *Collected Poems*. A kind of credo and prophecy, they are heralds to the saving grace (secular) of imagination, which binds fragments into unity, or love. The poetry that has followed has been the humble result of a humble struggle—the slow, dogged building of his final home, as may be seen in the increasing number of metaphors of enclosure in his recent poems. Day Lewis has written no more ambitious poems and no more truly original ones, but those which did follow *An Italian Visit* were no less "necessary poems," the rooms of some projected "ideal home."

CHAPTER 6

The Lyric Impulse

AS THE Charles Eliot Norton lecturer at Harvard in 1964–65, Day Lewis delivered a series of essays later published as *The Lyric Impulse*. Like *The Poetic Image* of nearly two decades earlier, the lectures define a commitment which had come increasingly to be Day Lewis' great obsession and his ultimate strategy for turning poetry away from intellect and back to the emotions—or better, from the public back to the personal. The lectures define what is in effect his own retrenchment, his return at last to the native element of poet-as-singer which he had sought in his earliest verse. It is not that his poetry of recent years is not mature or technically more successful than his earlier work: maturity has only confirmed Day Lewis' powers as an imitative poet, one whose style is more the product of his "tradition" than of experiment. It was a long way round from *Beechen Vigil* to *The Lyric Impulse* and the poems which group about it, through the intellectual poetry of the 1930's and the self-analyses of the 1940's. In his later poetry what he seems to have been seeking and has perhaps found is acceptance—or a kind of late innocence.

I *Poetic Grace*

The Lyric Impulse, a strikingly casual book, is almost completely void of intellectual tension. Because it follows Day Lewis' last three volumes of poems rather than emerging from the immediacy of their creation, its argument is a kind of afterthought and apology. Or rather, we find in it the ultimate emergence of the residual conviction that earlier had prevented him, on the one hand, from embracing a Marxist poetics and, on the other, from any kind of experimental daring. As such, the book is an unimpassioned and direct plea for another countercurrent in modern poetry: a return, as it were, to the primal origins of poetry in song and a repudiation of the self-conscious, intellectual tradition of modern poetry to which Day Lewis had earlier been party. This reaction is a common enough one in recent years; in fact, the desire for a return to simplicity, directness, the common idiom or oral tradition has taken a number of more vigorous forms (stylistic and philosophical) in the United States.[1] But Day Lewis' interest in the "lyrical impulse" is strangely atavistic—at once Romantic and anti-Romantic (or better, against the indulgence of personality in poetry). Ironically, the less cerebral his poetry becomes, the fewer spots of successful lyricism it contains.

The gist of Day Lewis' argument in *The Lyric Impulse* is that the history of poetry, especially its recent history, has been a progressive movement away from the roots of the poetic "impulse," the lyric or "singing" line, though here and there that line has survived and even been revitalized. Although he claims to be speaking about genre, he is really speaking about a mystique of ecstasy, or about inspiration as the muse. Spontaneity, youthfulness, innocence, renewal—these are the lyric qualities. Or, as he enumerates them, "Brevity, simplicity, purity" (5). Even in the 1930's this magic had possessed him, adding spirituality to his Marxist materialism. In *A Hope for Poetry*, he devoted a chapter to the "lyrical impulse" as that which moves every poet and "makes him write poetry rather than prose" (67). But, in spite of this deference to primal and pure simplicity (and its impersonality), he had serious reservations at the time about the possibility of the lyric impulse's surviving where self-consciousness "intervenes between the poet's moods and his poetry" (67). More significantly, he was disturbed, as noted earlier, by its "certain irresponsibility": "the lyric is a form of poetry, more than any other, within which the poet is answerable to nothing but its own laws and the experience of his senses" (67). Christopher Caudwell was quick to see the Lawrencean divergence even in passages which cautioned about the dangers of this necessary "impulse." For Day Lewis had to admit even then that the lyric impulse was his equivalent of the *élan vital* in poetry; and what he sought was a way of harnessing the life of poetry for communal ends.

Such concerns about the "irresponsibility" of the lyric impulse were understandable in the 1930's; yet even this temporizing about purity and impersonality provoked the hard-line Marxist censure of *A Hope for Poetry*. In *The Lyric Impulse*, Day Lewis is no longer answerable to immediate history but only to his inclinations and talents. The book builds from a rather cursory series of historical and stylistic perspectives on the "lyric" as genre to a culminating chapter called "The Golden Bridle" in which Day Lewis returns once again to the myth of Pegasus to argue for the lyric impulse as something like a "moment . . . of grace" and, sounding rather like Robert Graves, for the goddess of inspiration which lies in the unconscious. The argument is, in effect, Day Lewis' reprise on the last chapter of *The Poetic Image*, where he flirted with an archetypal theory of poetic causality as an explanation of poetry's universality and hence of its communal function. The vagaries of the argument aside, we must certainly conclude that Day Lewis is speaking at the tired end of more than thirty years of thinking about poetry and that he has had to confront its various failures as surrogate for religion, ideology, revelation, and—in both I. A. Richards' and F. R. Leavis' terms—morality. What remains is the function (although a part of its very limitation) of saving man from himself. The lyric impulse demands a surrender to experience by way of achieving, in the form-giving act of the song, a detachment and impersonality in regard to that experience. It bears one, Day Lewis argues in *Poetic Image,* through the chaos of personal confusion to the common ground of experience, merging the personal with those elemental or archetypal realities shared and sharable by all humanity (139).

The three slim volumes of poetry (*Pegasus and Other Poems*, 1957; *The Gate*, 1962; and *The Room*, 1965) Day Lewis had published since *An Italian Visit* are in a sense his own surrender to the lyric impulse, a surrender, that is to say, to what of the old instinctual energy remains. But conscious surrenders are rarely total. The single obsession of his late poetry is "love" (which he had come to think of in *The Poetic Image* as "a kind of necessity by which all things are bound together and in which, could the whole pattern be seen, their contradictions would appear reconciled" [37]) against death. As early as *A Hope for Poetry*, he argued that the root of all human impulse was love and that love could only flourish in a social environment which made intimate contact among individuals possible. The poet must live among friends and speak the language that bound him ultimately to his living unit. Love, in other words, is Day Lewis' metaphor (or euphemism?) for a kind of primal (hence elementally social) unity. Love is an escape from personality, from solipsism, into family and society; it is ultimately the root of all that is eternal, man's sense of the fundamental interrelation of all things, the basis of all laws of relation and unity. The late poems in their humble and self-limited way are attempts to isolate from time enduring moments—the cherished and secure past, a moment of love, the meaning of violence, a common yet recurrent experience such as departure or the journey which becomes the intimate archetype of life moving toward death. Poetry fixes the privileged moment in the larger pattern of human events, making both those moments and the events themselves eternal; it confirms the archetypes which subsume history's changes. It transforms time into the poetic image and, hence, into assumed universals.

In this context we can more clearly understand Day Lewis' definition of, and interest in, the lyric as "the purest and simplest form of poetry": "It is a poem which expresses a single state of mind, a single mood, or sets two simple moods one against the other" (*Lyric Impulse,* 3). It is the "instinctive spontaneity" in human song which is threatened by modern man's elaborate "self-consciousness" (4–5). To recall his earlier book, it is a "pure image": "This saying of only one thing at a time, without reservations, modifying parentheses, mental complications of any kind, is the lyric's chief term of reference" (5).

The lyric, to put it simply, is for Day Lewis an escape from history, the abstraction of experience into its transcendent and eternal perspective. The ultimate temporality of music is synchronic rather than diachronic. The lyric is the genre of innocence and, as Day Lewis' definition suggests, has seldom existed in its pure form. In fact, his title, stressing *Impulse*, celebrates the latent yet magical innateness of this energy which he unblushingly identifies with "grace." Though such energy rarely manifests itself directly and has suffered a variety of corruptions by intellect (the major one, significantly, in the divorce of lyric from music and in its evolution towards verbality and thought), it remains, nevertheless, the alembic without which the essential poetry is never distilled. The struggle of the modern poet to regain this purity from mind (or better, to submit mind's divisiveness to it) is, as it were, his struggle to be a poet—to possess the "golden bridle" of Pegasus and be transported by it. Day Lewis' earlier faith in the cohesive energy of mind, as celebrated in *Transitional Poem*, gives way to a new subjectivism.

The myth of Pegasus which Day Lewis had appropriated in *The Poetic Image* becomes once more his "image of the creative process" (*Lyric Impulse,* 10). Or, more precisely, it is his image of the poet's being possessed and redeemed from mind by the self-transcending powers of imagination. It is ironic that his effort to turn away from modernism and its self-conscious involvement in the processes of creation led Day Lewis halfway round to the modern once more. Self-consciousness will not let go of his own poems; the more they affect the simple spontaneity of the lyric impulse, the more they return to the old themes and compulsions: the trauma of departure or the fall from innocence, the inevitable journey through an alien environment, the instability of human relationships, and the skepticism of all resolutions except those of the poetic image. Day Lewis is not a purely lyrical poet, no more so in his later work than in his earlier; and so his poems turn out to be not pure lyrics but self-conscious speculations on lyric themes. The impurities with which, he argues, the mind has broken up the singing line of the original lyric remain at the center of his own poems: irony, self-conscious commentary, the overt moral. The pure image becomes metaphor, bearing its analogue of meaning to experience.

If the enervating conflict of modernism lies between the poet's desire to reinvoke the simple emotions and the complexities of a thought which will not trust simplicity, to use Day Lewis' own well-worn distinction, then his late poetry falls unceremoniously between the two. We might say that it yearns too powerfully for the purity of innocence, the simplicity of love, and the security of enclosed and remembered spaces. In other words, Day Lewis could not in the end face the consequences of his materialism, nor could he find an adequate belief in spirit—the "grace" of the lyrical impulse—to replace it.

II *The Golden Bridle*

While it would be wrong to say that *Pegasus and Other Poems* is dominated by the myth of its title, there is a sense in which the figure of Pegasus incorporates Day Lewis' "intentions" in his last three volumes. In *The Poetic Image*, he had made his first extensive reference to the myth as the figure of poetry's transformative power over chaos (99—100). A decade later, in the Henry Sedgwick Memorial Lecture at Cambridge, published as *The Poet's Way of Knowledge*, he returned to it as the metaphor of poetic inspiration, the "golden bridle" which became the superintending power of *The Lyric Impulse*. *The Poet's Way of Knowledge* is more or less contemporaneous with *Pegasus and Other Poems*. Thin though it is, the lecture is a revealing example of Day Lewis' continuing search for a "tradition" and for the kind of absolutes—stable ideas, sharable beliefs, and common language—needed by the poet to bulwark a relativistic world: "Poetry on the whole requires a stable foundation of ideas from which to make its flights: but today, and particularly in the all-important field of physics, there seems to be a constant modification and readjustment of scientific theory" (29). The inevitable answer would be neo-Romantic (the assumed unity of human subjectivity), projecting a social community of poet and audience based on simplicity and on the intimate relation of selves to environment. Day Lewis would find an escape from personality by transforming unique personal experience into everyman's. The lyric impulse generalizes the private emotion into its communal forms. It is the poet's task "to show the momentousness of life's most common-place happenings" (30). Like William Carlos Williams' "No ideas but in things," Day Lewis' remarks imply a world without a center, or meaning. And if he did not, like Williams, see that such a position demanded a complete departure from the tradition in both style and language, he nonetheless recognized the consequences of dismissing the sublime and the transcendent.

Day Lewis' interpretation of the Pegasus myth has some interesting ramifications which are only partly explained by the traditional role of the myth. For, if Pegasus is the classical figure of a transcending energy (hence inspiration) to Bellerophon's earth-bound consciousness, Day Lewis' symbol is somewhat less sublime: he is both "brute" and "angel" as the title poem has it (*Pegasus*, 10). More important, the "golden" or "magic bridle" becomes not simply the gratuitous transport of inspiration but a kind of release, a form of "grace" received only at the expense of strenuous discipline. In short, the transport of Pegasus can only follow the most concentrated discipline of energies. "A bridle both restrains energy and releases it," Day Lewis writes in *The Lyric Impulse*, "disciplines and directs: there are times (and they tend to come in the early stages of composition, I find) when a poet must exercise stern control lest the poem run away with him; there are times when he can let the reins lie loose" (132). And he then evokes Valéry's argument that strict form is necessary to keep the poem from saying everything, and hence nothing; thus, he argues for form as that which not only restrains but also stimulates. (In his most recent book of poems, *The Room*, Day Lewis includes a short piece called "On Not Saying Everything.")

Valéry's formalism aside, we can more clearly understand Day Lewis' mystique of the poet's privileged moment in terms of restraint rather than of stimulation. The poems of recent years are anything but visionary breakthroughs, or even lyrics of innocence; they are, instead, the products of a disciplined reduction of experience to abstraction or to the substance of metaphorical insights. *Pegasus*, for instance, is divided into three main parts: (1) four poems, including the title one, based on Greek myth; (2) a section of dedicatory, elegiac, and semi-satiric poems; and (3) a sequence of poems based on memories. He maintains this rather obvious distribution of themes in his subsequent two books, separating, as in *The Room*, personal (confessional or nostalgic) poems from those treating "others." The convenience of his orderly arrangements bespeaks his dependence on poetry as a way of containing, as opposed to transforming, the atoms of personal experience within the archetypal categories which make them appear universal. His journeys are no longer experienced ones, nor does the poetry manifest the urgency and immediacy of departure, dislocation, movement, or arrival. The maturity and the unstimulating sameness of Day Lewis' last poems are the pyrrhic victory of the poet over his self-doubts and the almost total submission of his material to a desired order.

The "mythic" poems of *Pegasus* are good examples of Day Lewis' discreetly self-imposed limitations. They are, in large part, rather conventional reductions of myths to moral reference or to thematic convenience. "Ariadne on Naxos" (18) assumes the form of dramatic monologue, in which the woman is the embodiment of emotion and hence the manifestation of the imagination as opposed to the divisive "complexities" of the male mind. "Baucis and Philemon" (14) exhibits something of Day Lewis' interest in the particularity of the epical line and in a low-keyed, descriptive, pastoral poetry. The preoccupation of the poem with death and metamorphosis is an all-too-obvious appeal to the unitive and hence transformative power of love—and thus to the immortality of art. But "Pegasus" (7) is the most obvious homage to the primacy of the emotions and to the self-re-creative powers of imagination. The poem, however, fails to rise above the obvious allegory of the myth, except that Day Lewis maneuvers it to express the rhythms of his own struggle with the muse:

> That furious art, the pursuer's rhythmic pace
> Failed in him now. Another self had awoken,
> Which knew—but felt no chagrin, no disgrace—
> That he, not the winged horse, was being broken:
> It was his lode, his lord, his appointed star,
> He but its shadow and familiar.

In the poem's extended metaphor, Day Lewis works out the marriage of myth and the contemporary dilemma—the poet's necessary submission to "dream" wherein is given the "magic bridle" that "you yourself made." The bridle, the "grace" of discipline, is the creative channeling of "brute" energies; but the poem's "moral" lies in its mixed metaphor. If the "bridle" is given to him in "sleep," that is, by his submission to feeling and dream, he is nonetheless the maker of it in that it is the form (both the tradition he inherited and his self-discipline) that has mastered his energies and given the name. Sleep is a state of impersonality, an escape from consciousness, and a merging of self with the universal mind. The "magic bridle," or imagination, is the "supernature" of man who transcends himself by submitting to his essentially human powers. And Pegasus is the name of that supernature, its form—or, in other words, Pegasus is a metaphor for poetry itself. But this particular poem cannot, in the end, marry the myth with any plausible system of explanation—religious, mystical, psychological—and hence insists on the myth as simply a figure of the poet's faith.

The mythic poems, in short, are evidence of Day Lewis' inability to escape the disbelief of his earlier materialism. The myth of Pegasus is an abstraction, or a "system" of explanation—a vehicle for talking about the otherwise felt processes of inspiration and imaginative act. The book's middle section consists of thirteen rather indifferent short poems, ranging from satiric pieces of an obvious kind, like "The Committee," to Hardyesque imitations, like "Almost Human" (30), and includes Day Lewis' late variation on Frost's "The Road Not Taken," called "The Wrong Road" (27). These poems are neither emotionally taut nor emotionally elevated, and they show little evidence of being touched by the "grace" of any "magic bridle." The Frostian poem, for example, dissipates the tensions of Frost's choice and thus his acceptance, and it ends in a dull moral of accommodation: the inevitable giving in to "necessity" which is the product of Day Lewis' inescapable materialism.

Elegies for Meredith and Dylan Thomas are poignant, but only in the book's last section does Day Lewis achieve his authentic late voice—in his reengagement with the past, his return to the "buried day." What he seeks is the security of a completed space, the remembered "house" of his past, the home in which the family once existed as a secure and harmonious unit. That past is the space of a faded memory, a space that now must be imaginatively refurnished—that is, it must be transposed into the total form of poetry, the "poetic image." And so the creating of poems becomes an act whereby the poet reconstitutes his beginning in his end and therein achieves the order away from which his life has led and toward which he has been driven.

Only if seen in this sense do the nostalgic poems of Part Three escape the charge of sentimentalism. "The House Where I Was Born" (43) carefully exploits this metaphor of the disappearing past:

> An elegant, shabby, white-washed house
> With a slate roof. Two rows
> Of tall sash windows. Below the porch, at the foot of
> The steps, my father, posed
> In his pony trap and round clerical hat.
> This is all the photograph shows.

The prosaic rhythm and precise, uncolored images are apt. The poet's commerce with the past begins with his exposure to its bare, lifeless structure; the relationships of the photograph (like his memory of an earlier self) center upon the figure of barren order, the father.

Revealingly, the poet's search is for the mother and for the vital room in which she gave birth to him. He seeks the moment of his origin, the enlivened space out from which his life progressively had led—from primal order to isolation, the fall. The conflict of father and son and the son's loss of his mother have easily traced biographical origins (see *Buried Day, passim*); and they submit, of course, to obvious psychological interpretations. Moreover, this very photograph and his speculations upon it serve to introduce Day Lewis' autobiography, his attempt to recapture his "buried" self (16). But the structural quality of this poem makes it more than ordinary; for the photograph of the house and father renders a series of lifeless images: shabby, colorless, and rigidly circular. The father's "round clerical hat" is the focal center of a rigid, formally composed, and hence dead world. The poet struggles to revitalize this space, to animate it, to find the room in which he was born—a room in which both mother and father are present:

> I know that we left you before my seedling
> Memory could root and twine
> Within you. Perhaps that is why so often I gaze
> At your picture, and try to divine
> Through it the buried treasure, the lost life—
> Reclaim what was yours, and mine.

And the poem ends in images of reimagined warmth:

> I put up the curtains for them again
> And light a fire in their grate:
> I bring the young father and mother to lean above me,
> Ignorant, loving, complete:
> I ask the questions I never could ask them
> Until it was too late.

Memory and passion revitalize the photograph's empty structure with heat and youth—with love. Thus the Whitmanesque scene becomes "complete" and, in contrast to the cold photograph, alive. The imagination, in touching its origins, the roots of its vitality, reconfirms itself. It rediscovers its innocence and its purity, and thus it comes to know the meaning of its decline. The questions it is privileged to ask are, presumably, of the mystery of primal order—the unity it has known only as something lost, the unity embodied in the living relation of mother and father and their bond of love. For the primordial center, the lost origin, is figured as an original relationship or marriage. Imagination alone brings mother and father to lean once more over the child—thus composing an ideal relationship, the family. The process of the poem, moving into the past, arrives at the eternal moment from which all history has moved and to which the self in time desires to return. The poet, that is, brings once more to the cold, imperial, paternal reason of history a warm, vital, maternal unreason which is his imagination.

Two subsequent poems, "Father to Sons" and "Son and Father," make similar explorations of the past and the discord of hierarchical or generational relationships, seeking the "house" of an earlier self and finding only the chill of a space in which the father-authority is not complemented by the vitality of the mother. The relation of father to son is a metaphor of history, of discontinuity, and thus of the death of warmth and passion by the hand of consciousness—of innocence by guilt. The poems which conclude *Pegasus* are filled with nostalgia for the warm rooms of childhood, and particularly for the room of birth wherein, as in "Christmas Eve" (48), the imagination might be reborn, or, as in "Dedham Vale, Easter, 1954" (56), might realize a "paradise vale where all is/ Movement and all at peace."

But Day Lewis remains a divided self—and a divided poet—torn between a willed innocence and an unremitting skepticism. The "Moods of Love" (59)—the book's major poem, a sonnet sequence—indulges the illusory dream of innocence; but the ecstasy of moods depends upon a Keatsian double perspective, a negative capability. Unfortunately, Day Lewis' own negative capability does not afford him the Keatsian range of beauty within terror, but it is nevertheless the dialectic of illusion and skepticism, dream and history, out of which his last poems are composed:

> Two are reborn as one: where all is passing
> They dream a now for ever and set fair.

Reborn! The very word is like a bell.
From the warm trance, the virgin arms awoken,
Each turns to his sole self. Out of the shell
They step, unchanged. Only a spell is broken.
Though there's no cure, no making whole, no fusion,
Live while you can the merciful illusion.

III *Stylized Game*

There has been no substantial development since *Pegasus*. The titles of Day Lewis' last two books of poems, *The Gate* and *The Room*, are metaphorically indicative of a poetry overwhelmed by deliberate limitation. The titles describe in a sense the kinds of desperate reduction Day Lewis was willing to make in order to achieve some kind of wholeness or order or perfection—some kind of perspective upon himself as person and upon his role, so often to himself problematic, as a man of letters. The books are filled with images of restricted space, spaces in which the imagination at last has control over the matter surrounding it. They are images, that is, of a poetic or artistically ordered space—of atomistic worlds finally composed, but only at the expense of severe reduction and at times ruthless condensation.

Perhaps the most revealing of all Day Lewis' late poems is the one mentioned earlier as being inspired by Valéry, "On Not Saying Everything" (*Room*, 10). There is a general gloss on it in *The Lyric Impulse* (149), but the poem itself is more unblushingly confessional than the critic suggests. It opens with a metaphor of a tree which is defined by its own organic laws. No matter the size it grows to be, the tree is defined by its structure and condemned to be tree; its fate lies in its origin, the laws of its seed. But likewise its identity lies there. This law applies also to poetry, as stanza two forthrightly states:

> Unwritten poems loom as if
> They'd cover the whole of earthly life.
> But each one, growing, learns to trim its
> Impulse and meaning to the limits
> Roughed out by one, then more defined
> In its own truth's expanding light.
> A poem, settling to its form,
> Finds there's no jailer, but a norm
> Of conduct, and a fitting sphere
> Which stops it wandering everywhere.

Despite poetry's potentially mystical infiniteness ("its own truth's expanding light"), the stress remains on its "norm." The poem's metaphors are of severely reduced space, composition by compression: "trim/ Its impulse," "modified . . . expanding light," "fitting sphere." And, the poem concludes, like poetry, like love:

> Each to his own identity,
> Grown back, shall prove our love's expression
> Purer for this limitation.
> Love's essence, like a poem's shall spring
> From the not saying everything.

The style of Day Lewis' last poems is similarly a quest for limitation, a "norm/ Of conduct" achieved only by self-conscious discipline and crippling imitation. The title poem of *The Gate*, for example, maneuvers the image of the "gate" as the compositional center of a picture wherein order is the triumph of art over life. The "gate," the "dead-centre" of a pictorial landscape, never opens; but all nature exists only relative to it. In this field of natural images, the gate is the only artifice, the man-made center—"dead-centre." The poem is not the scene of a "human event" but of order achieved at the expense of change. The gate is an image of the mind's categorical discipline (separating fields), placed in a scene (a picture) that is itself a work of art. Or, in other words, the focal image of the gate within a field of natural images makes the created order central. Nature depends on man's order, as he depends on its order. There is no opening in this field, no flow; for art triumphs over process by taking process into its field, giving it a center.

The poems of *The Gate* are calculatedly self-limited; the poet in the poems is ultimately the creature as well as the creator of the space he occupies, condemned to his "View From an Upper Window" (13). His "prospect" of reality has the virtue of limitation; his freedom is what he can do within necessity. The "prospect" from the open window is distorted and obscured, and he lives in the perpetual anticipation of what he "might" make of it. But his ultimate consolation is that his freedom is his limitation: "Perhaps I should think about the need for frames." For within "frames," like the restrictions of poetic form, the poet makes the "fragment" yield the "whole/ Without spilling over into imbecility." Thus cosmos is the reality of limitation:

> Each of them [frames], though limited its choice, reclaims
> Some terra firma from the chaos. Who knows?—
> Each of *us* may be set here, simply to compose
> From a few grains of universe a finite view,

> By One who occasionally needs such frames
> To look at his boundless creation through?

The Gate displays the poverty rather than the plentitude of an order achieved by "such frames." We need not say that Day Lewis is incorrect in acknowledging that poetic form, as a kind of limitation, is also the essence of freedom—that the vital lies in intensity rather than dispersal. His error is in making this concept a creed and in refusing his imagination the privilege of taking chances. His formalism is not Valéry's, no matter how Day Lewis embraces that "ancestor." Nor is it Frost's, whose figure of the poem is a series of progressive choices (like the road not taken) which increasingly commit the poet to a form and thereby free him by restricting his freedom—though Frost is another favorite "ancestor." Only the 1930's, by disabusing Day Lewis of the immediate past, had thrust his imagination toward futures; and even that thrust, we now see, was based on a pastoral myth and on a circular journey. Returning home to a more secure order in his late poems, Day Lewis submits to the lesson of "Sheepdog Trials in Hyde Park" (17), which incidentally he dedicated to Frost, and consolidates his gains. Order is achieved by reducing life (and the writing of poems) to a "stylized game":

> What's needfully done in the solitude of sheep-runs—
> Those tough, real tasks—becomes this stylized game,
> A demonstration of intuitive wit
> Kept natural by the saving grace of error.
> To lift, to fetch, to drive, to shed, to pen
> Are acts I recognize, with all they mean
> Of shepherding the unruly, for a kind of
> Controlled woolgathering is my work too.

The creative act, Day Lewis has come to see, is an act of containment, of order set against chaos, life against death. But paradoxically, the will to order is its own dream of death. It is not unfair to observe that Day Lewis' poetic talents have suffered the fate of the caged, "abdicated beast" he laments in "Circus Lion": "Not anger enough left—no, nor despair—/ To break his teeth on the bars." (*Gate*, 19). Day Lewis has made his own cage and cannot live without bars. There are poems in *The Gate* which might once have been animated by anger or despair—but the motif is now accommodation. Interviewing Frost in 1957, Day Lewis managed to entice the old poet to re-interpret his chief maxim, that poetry ends in a clarification of life, into a poetics of accommodation, an engagement of confusion which ends in the clarity of the short view.[2] Another part of the interview touched upon Frost's penchant for narrative and on his interest in people speaking, in the "gossip" of the common man. This democratization of poetry, said Day Lewis, is modern man's substitute for "hero-worship," and Frost agreed. We might rather call it the vestiges of sentimental humanism—the need to discover the superhuman in the human, the extraordinary in what modern man has left: the ordinary. The poems of *The Gate* stand as testimony to this form of hero worship: the heroism of submission to necessity.

The poems in *The Room* are more or less confirmations, adjustments to the room of self and its place in the house of society. Almost equally divided between their attention to "Fables and Confessions" (personal lyrics) and "Others" (occasional poems, including an elegy for Churchill and a touching piece on Jacqueline Kennedy's suffering during the moment of the assassination, called "Pietà"), the poems are attempts to compose a poetic world in which violence is contained, suffering is transcended, and the self comes to terms with itself by accepting as final its present "room." If Day Lewis' youthful poems are of departure, of moving in and moving out, changing homes and outgrowing the present, his last are fittingly of tidying the little space the poet has left. The title poem and another called "Saint Anthony's Shirt" (17) are the logical end of a journey.

In "The Room," dedicated to George Sefaris, Day Lewis commemorates the poet's retreat into the rooms of memory (into the windowless room of his "real" self). "Saint Anthony's Shirt" is a touching acceptance of the room of his body—"wasting and renewing cell by cell"—in which he must function, still seeking the "master thread" that will make the "patchwork, piecemeal self" whole. He is, in short, still in search of identity, which is only available in the process of being, not in some essence. Once more Day Lewis turns to the communal as against the personal solution, to the love in which one is most uniquely himself "when I become another":

> Tending a sick child, groping my way into
> A woman's heart, lost in a poem, a cause,
> I touched the marrow of my being, unbared
> Through self-oblivion. Nothing remains so true
> As the outgoingness. This moving house
> Is home, and my home, only when it is shared.

If we look closely at the structure of his figures and pass over the obvious implications of love as a form of self-annihilation, we note that the "room" in which Day Lewis finds himself is a social or communal space where action takes place. It is an analogue of the poem, in which the poet is lost in order to find himself—the poem in which, by giving to others as a gesture of love, he confirms form upon his being, and manifests it communally. To be, then, is communal, is "outgoingness." This confession he seems to make about why he still needs to write poems, long after his voice has lost any originality it may have had. Poetry is his only escape from the tomb of subjectivity into the eternally ongoing community of others, as well as his investment in the continuum of his tradition. And this view helps to explain why the writing of poems remains necessary, long after originality is possible. "Home" is something "shared"—a self realized only when given to an "other" or a poem made and given to others. Or to recall the dominant figure of the last book, a "room" is to live in.

CHAPTER 7

The Poetics of Hope

LITERARY history will know Day Lewis as a contemporary man of letters, which, alas, means a dabbler in many things, an expert in none. He is, of course, a poet before anything else, a minor poet in the best sense of that phrase; and whatever reputation he has as a poet seems more the result of historical accident than of individual genius. He is a poet of the 1930's, the "Auden Group," of "Macspaunday," and though he has long since given up his allegiance to causes and groups, he has not really survived his "group" role nor become a force in modern poetry.

It is only in the past century that history has acted so conveniently to divide literary periods into decades—the 1920's; the 1930's; and, going back to the 1890's, the "mauve decade." But of these periods, only the 1930's seems to have been determinant of its literature rather than the literature determinant of how we know the decade. The myths of the 1920's are those of its literature—or quasi-myths which were created by quasi-historians, especially in America, to conform with the clichés of a "jazz age," "lost generation," and the youthful innocence of "only yesterday." In almost every respect, the diversity and vitality of its art is our mirror of the decade. We can talk about the characteristic fiction or poetry of the 1920's as experimental, revolutionary, formalistic, avantgarde, or modernistic; but, above all, it was not a monolithic literature. Whether literary history is right or wrong in this regard, the literature of the 1930's seems defined by a historically monolithic preoccupation; and poets-of-the-1930's are just that—not individuals. In the cases especially of Auden and Day Lewis, the time encouraged a poetics of impersonality and catered to their essentially communal interests.

I The Necessary Myth

Yet poets are individuals, and rarely are they the willing pawns of history. Those of the 1930's we recognize today are the ones who survived the decade, as did Auden, or who, like Dylan Thomas and E. E. Cummings, challenged its ideological communalism with the stylistic idiosyncrasies of absolute individualism. The thing which made Auden the premier poet of the age is that he was both its analyst and synthesist; he both confirmed and transcended its style, probed its illnesses and convulsions, and by staying imaginatively alive, escaped its death-dealing anonymity. Impersonality for Auden was the ability to identify with others, other positions, alien philosophies, and the like, without yielding to any one of them as final truth.

Day Lewis was not so plastic as Auden, but neither was he a serf of history. In a very real sense, we can now say that his poetry was an effort not to accommodate to history but to redeem it and thus to redeem his poetic self which admittedly was conditioned by it. The seemingly homogeneous art we call "the poetry of the 1930's," with its strategies of impersonality and its longing for consummate futures, turns out to be in each particular case a desperate struggle to preserve the self. And this meant conserving a defined, coherent tradition. What appeared to be the one voice of "Macspaunday" is really four voices directed at the same historical crisis. What gradually emerged was the individual nuance of each response: four very different poets with four distinctly different responses to their reality. And yet, because these were socially committed poets, who identified, if in diverse ways, their individual crises with their culture's, attention was directed more at the common conditions they faced than at the style with which they faced them.

Day Lewis, however, was, as we have noted, a more consciously imitative poet than Auden, Spender, or MacNeice—not simply because he was less original, but because he found imitation essential to his search for an individual, yet impersonal, style. In this sense he may be considered a representative poet of the decade, for in his own modest experiments we find a comprehensive awareness not only of what the poet must do but what the more daring ones were doing. From the vantage of more than a quarter century, we can now see that they were doing essentially what poets do in every period of crisis: they were concerned with discovering a poetry which would engage the present by redeeming (not consecrating) the past. The difference for the twentieth century, however, was that the past no longer seemed worthy of redeeming. The revolutions of the age had wiped away metaphysical coherence and replaced it with the fragmented teleologies of depth psychology, logical positivism, and dialectical materialism, the most illusively comprehensive of all because it married faith and politics. The problem of finding a poetics which would incorporate these new "absolutes" in a new "myth" Day Lewis later described in *Poetic Image* as the poet's task to generate "the myth of the individual" to replace the "great educative myths" of the "collective mind" (32)—by which he meant that the poet was responsible for re-discovering the emotional community of men which had once been, at least as metaphysical nostalgia held it, manifest in history.

To put it another way, we can now see that poets like Day Lewis were not seeking a poetics to conform to a new ideology (in this case, Marxism) but were trying through poetry to find the recurrently human "myths" that any new ideology (especially one that links past and future) must incorporate if it is to serve human need. Poetry, Day Lewis discovered, must engage ideology, not be subsumed by it. Poetics derived from the educative myths by which man advances from darkness to light; but poetry also created, or constituted, those myths. Day Lewis' apparent embrace of Marxism may well be interpreted as a desperate grabbing on to the only coherent faith the decade offered. But the particular ideology was ultimately irrelevant; and, when its historical manifestations made it no longer sufficient to sustain the poet's emotional "hope," his poetry continued as before to serve him as an instrument by which the present self relates itself to the changeless human community, the eternal past. Day Lewis is not the same poet today he was in the 1930's, but he continues to ask essentially the same things from poetry. And, if his poetics has undergone substantial changes in degree, it has been thematically consistent over some forty years.

II *Marxian Pastoral*

For each of the three major periods of his career, Day Lewis produced one significant critical statement: *A Hope for Poetry* (1934), *The Poetic Image* (1947), and *The Lyric Impulse* (1965). Those three books, along with a modest number of relevant essays, constitute a not exactly original body of criticism which appears, on the surface at least, to have carried Day Lewis far from his beginnings. But, like the more obvious changes in his poetic style, his critical position only disguises its consistency by altering its perspectives. A number of the critical positions he advocated earlier, which appeared to be the result of historical pressures, reoccur in an altogether different context later, not so much changed as refined and simplified. There is in his criticism, as

in his poetry, a gradual but persistent retreat from history to self, from
society to the community of minds and hearts; but, if the perspective
alters, the values remain constant. For from the beginning, community
was nothing more than fundamental human relationships—the family.
There is almost nothing in his later criticism that is not in *A Hope for
Poetry* and in the poetry for which it stands as apology. The particular
admixture of Marxism and Eliotic traditionalism, not to say of
Lawrence and Freud, makes that essay one of the most revealing poetic
documents of the 1930's.

A Hope for Poetry is historically conditioned, certainly, but its
argument is not limited to its time. In one very important sense, it is a
sustained attack on "pure poetry" by a poet who sensed in himself
distinct leanings in that direction.[1] The essay is, then, an equally
sustained argument for a social poetry, or better, for a poetry of social
relevance—a poetry of "community." The "hope" is based, to be sure,
on an apparent contradiction: while, on the one hand, it affirms the
poet's need of tradition, it argues, on the other, for a revolution in
poetry—and hence for the poet as celebrant of new visions, new
frontiers, new communities. Day Lewis himself recognized the contradiction in stating that the fundamental issue for any poet of that time
was whether man should change himself (the "change of heart" motif)
so as to change society, or whether he should embrace the idea of a new
society which in turn would make new men (47). On the simpler level
of the poet as self, his argument reflects more logically the conflict
between individualism and the tradition, Romanticism and humanism.
Day Lewis, like any true poet, insisted, of course, on straddling
categories; and the fact that he later described his position as "romantic
humanism" offers us less clarity of definition than it does evidence of
his desire to roll the world into one comprehensible ball.

But the fundamental issues of tradition and of the individual talent
are contemplated in *A Hope for Poetry* within a context both
historically and ideologically different from Eliot's. The book opens
with a brief chapter on the nature and the need of tradition, using the
characteristic and revealing image of the journey (of the younger son
far from home) for the periodic countermovements in the English
poetic tradition. Day Lewis' point is quite clear: any revolutionary
departure from the tradition is by definition made in terms of that
tradition; his own group, worshiping its immediate "ancestor"—Hopkins, Eliot, and Wilfred Owen—is only fulfilling the poet's basic need of
a "link with the past" from which he draws "power and refreshment"
(3). Hopkins, Eliot, and Owen are not only ancestors and links to the

tradition but "revolutionaries": their experiments of style are heralds of a new turn in the tradition, yet deliberate appropriations of the past. This style fits a world in convulsive change, yet it confirms the profound order that survives change. Revolutionaries are the caretakers of any tradition, Day Lewis argues, for the vitality of tradition is in its processes, its changes and alterations.

Day Lewis thus manages to integrate traditionalism and dialectical materialism, and he does so in a way remarkably consistent with Marx but not with the Communist ideology of the 1930's. In the din of 1930's propaganda, it was difficult to recall the traditionalist base of dialectical materialism, in which revolution was not a breakoff from the past so much as the process of accommodating past to present by directing both toward the future. The process was one of purification and renewal—but, most important, it was process itself. As Georg Lukacs has said, "Those who do now know Marxism at all or know it only superficially or at second-hand, may be surprised by the respect for the classical heritage of mankind which one finds in the really great representatives of this doctrine and by their incessant references to that classical heritage."[2] Whatever Day Lewis' philosophical command of Marxism at the time, the materialistic commitment he and Auden made in the Preface to *Oxford Poetry, 1927*, was not unreconcilable with dialectical materialism.

The key passage, written by Day Lewis, of that Preface opted for environment as the crucial force in the evolution of values; and, in spite of the calculated obscurity of the argument, it is remarkably compatible with Marx's theory of the materialistic basis of consciousness. The problem for the poet was how to change that environment so that he could be changed by it—the answer was, inevitably, to discover the latent force of purity (and hence, innocence) in society and to ally oneself in community with it. That element, of course, was what remained of the old tribal or pastoral culture, the yeoman proletariat. Once again, Day Lewis' affinity for the English rustic life, as against the city-dwelling bourgeoisie, was easily adaptable to Marxist theory. *A Hope for Poetry* is in search of tradition quite simply because the poet needs one: a traditional audience, a communal language. Lacking that in the larger sense, however, precisely because it was the evolutionary schisms of society that had produced the modern crisis, the poet had to find its substitute in a coherent social group:

Now a compact, working social group has the same advantage for a poet as tradition: it enables him to take a number of things for granted.

He is aware instinctively of the average radius of individual experience and imagination, and he can use this knowledge in that task which Wordsworth pronounced to be one of the best services in which a writer can be engaged, the task of producing or enlarging the capability of men's minds for being excited. It is noticeable that the greatest achievements of poetry and the most prolific periods of poetry have arisen in small, compact, homogeneous communities such as the Greek city state or Elizabethan England. Where the community is swollen, spiritually disorganized and heterogeneous; where there is no widely accepted system of morals and no clearly defined circumference . . . the poet's data are terribly confused and his task correspondingly difficult. In the face of this intolerable complexity, the sensitive individual feels compelled to retire upon himself, to create artifically for himself a world of manageable proportions. . . . This act—a kind of starting again at the beginning—is being performed in post-war poetry. . . . The poet now is seeking to find and establish that central calm, a point from which he may begin to work outward again; and in the process he is bound to be obscure, for he is talking to himself and to his friends—to that tiny, temporarily isolated unit with which communication is possible, with whom he can take a certain number of things for granted. (*Hope for Poetry*, 36—37)

Self-consciously aware that this argument allies him with the obscurantists of modernism, who chose to speak to an elite audience rather than to dilute their art, Day Lewis insists that the poet's learning first to speak to a "group of friends" is as temporary as a new beginning. Here is the rationale for what critics scornfully called the "boy-scout element" in Day Lewis' and Auden's early work, with its private allusions and in-group humor. This was, for Day Lewis at least, prelude to a new poetic revival—the expansion of the working social group into the nucleus of a larger community and ultimately of a new society. There is an unremitting idealism in this "hope": "We shall not begin to understand postwar poetry until we realize that the poet is appealing above all for the creation of a society in which the real and living contact between man and man may again become possible. That is why, speaking from the living unit of himself and his friends, he appeals for the contraction of the social group to a size at which human contact may again be established and demands the destruction of all impediments to love" (38).

But the "hope" of a new beginning is one thing; the "new world," another. Day Lewis' "hope" is funded, if not upon the moral superiority of the artist, then upon his superior visionary stamina; he suggests that it is his (and his group's) change of heart which will begin the alteration of the environment that will in turn change society. More realistically, he views poetry as the sole remaining bridge—religion having failed—between the multiple schisms of modern man: the division of intellect and emotion (represented by the respective poetics of Wyndham Lewis and D. H. Lawrence) which are socially manifest in the urbanization of a technical society. Day Lewis' concern over the modern poet's need to find the language of a technological age is basically a concern that he discover the myths of that age—for, when he touches the myths, whose patterns are mirrors of emotional coherence, he will find the human and hence communal order beneath the appearances of disorder and alienation. He will speak of the social realities in a way that will touch the communal heart: "The revolutionary poet is not a leader: he stands, like a mirror at the crossroads, showing the traffic, the danger, the way you have come and the ways you may go—'your own divided heart' " (50). But this is not really as daring or as individualistic as Trotsky: "Personal lyrics of the very smallest scope," Trotsky wrote, "have an absolute right to exist within the new art. Moreover, the new man cannot be formed without a new lyric poetry. But to create it, the poet must feel the world in a new way."[3]

Though Christopher Caudwell was one of the harshest critics of the Auden Group, there is in *A Hope for Poetry* something of Caudwell's Marxism, if not his aggressive daring in giving the poet a new myth-making (Caudwell would call it "history-forming") role. For the key to Day Lewis' poetics and to the intellectual Marxism he shared with his peers is their fear of a nostalgia for a past, which indeed haunted them, with its deceptive security and its ultimate failure to sustain the good life. That past embodied the ideal of community and, in a specific sense, a kind of pastoral community based on the relations of man to man through his immediate contact with a common and intimate soil. It is revealing that Day Lewis would pay homage to the Romantics (and especially to Wordsworth), for their antiurban pastoralism while ignoring their (youthful at least) radical individualism and that he would condemn his immediate ancestors, the Georgians, for ignoring the discomforts of historical reality altogether while indulging their dubious talent for reducing everything to a pastoral idyl.

The antiurbanism of *A Hope for Poetry* (though more the result of pastoral nostalgia than of ideological conviction) coincided just as perfectly with Marx's fundamental theory of the class struggle, the bourgeois subjugation of the country by the town, as it did with Lawrencean vitalism. And, while Day Lewis insists the modern poet cannot ignore the technological present, he argues, on the other hand, that the poet cannot draw upon the thematic and imagistic resources of technological reality until they have been absorbed into the general consciousness and hence taken on the emotional coloration of natural life.[4] In other words, the responsibility of the poet is to assist in this accommodation of modern social reality to man's mythic needs. Paradoxically, he must assist society in acquiring the mythic language of its reality so that he can later draw upon that common resource, so that he can take it for granted: "The poet makes timeless legends out of our mortal, savage dust; and can also give blood and bones to a myth" (76). But he must have it both ways—the poet gives so that he can take, makes myths so that he can draw upon their communal power.

The social necessity of poetry, as *A Hope for Poetry* assesses it, is to accommodate its responsibility to the present world with its roots in tradition—and the English tradition of poetry for Day Lewis is essentially pastoral and lyric. His most passionate hope for poetry is not that it will eradicate the primitive in man but that it would conserve those vital roots which precede consciousness and history. In the end, Day Lewis could not be a Marxist; for, while he shared the Marxist faith in the material origins of consciousness and hence the primitive roots of society, he could not abide faith in ceaseless process and progressive consciousness. Where the Marxist, like Caudwell, stressed the evolution of poetry as consonant with the processes of history, Day Lewis' faith was in its ultimately conservative nature. Poetry never really changed, as Eliot had insisted; its revolutions of style merely conserved and confirmed the tradition. It denied the apocalyptic nature of Marxism. For Day Lewis, the future of poetry lay in its incessant return to its origins; poetry confirmed the eternal and the supernatural in man. Poetry for him is strictly metaphorical, a living transcription in the emotional rhythm of the word and line of immutable human truths that are untouched by historical process. Despite his fundamental materialism, Day Lewis could not really believe that environment was the primary cause of value; what he truly held was that basic values, like basic needs, had developed in a primal environment out of primordial human relationships. That environment was identified with the remote pastoral (hence ideal) past.

As inflexible as Eliot, Day Lewis set poetry against the reality of historical process; but unlike Eliot, he had no access to a "system" of belief which could adequately subsume process. And that lack, indeed, would appear to be the efficient cause of what original poetry (even that stylistically derivative from Auden) he wrote: his work in the

1930's. For the 1930's offered a severe challenge to his native conservatism, and it forced him again and again to confront the dynamics of historical change as a reality which denied the possibility of redeeming the past. Dialectical materialism, though it paid fit honor to the past, was not nostalgic. But, if Day Lewis became, as he later said, a "future-fan," it was not really as a believer in the Marxist apocalypse. He was able to find within the Marxian ideal of a new community a reforming of the pastoral ideal. His view of history was ultimately circular, not linear or dialectical. But his being thrown so rudely into the contemporary scene did have the positive effect of forcing him to recognize its challenges. They brought him face-to-face with the inadequacy of any "system," but did not allay his need of a "system." The particular tension in his early poetry derives from the pull of past and future against the present because the experience of modern reality must be accommodated to some mythic order—the journey away from became the journey toward, the magnetic mountain being the same to all men who live in time and aspire to transcend themselves.

III   *The Nostalgia of Wholeness*

The ease with which Day Lewis could pass from an apparently humanist poetics to an apparently new critical poetics has been explained all too easily in historical terms. Ideological disillusionment and the advent of war did not make a modern poet of him, no more than it sent him reeling backward from his modernist "ancestors" (Hopkins, Eliot, Owen) to his Victorian "ancestors" (Hardy and Meredith). Reviewing the very recent *Selected Poems*,[5] John Wain has charged that Day Lewis' only period as an original voice issued in *Word Over All* and that, before and after, his poetry was built on a series of imitations. What is more to the point is that the immediate post-1930's years left Day Lewis not without a theme (those never really altered) but without any larger context—an ideological or metaphysical "system"—in which to give those themes mythic substance. It was then he found the themes (for example, the journey) to be sufficient unto themselves and to be universal because they were recurrently human. Marxian universality gave way to archetypal universality—which is to say, diachronic history was replaced by synchronic history.

His study, *The Poetic Image*, is largely a confirmation of that discovery. It offers a poetics subsumed not by metaphysical or psychological systems (though it flirts with both, especially a theory of the collective consciousness which, in contrast to Jung's collective unconscious and like Eliot's simultaneous tradition, is subject to history's impressions though not to radical changes) but by man's shared and sharable emotional experience. Day Lewis no longer looked to historical process for his universals; they were discoverable only in the poetic process, that abstracting power which touches the eternal (form) with the temporal (flow). History for Day Lewis is the discontinuity of particular events or ages subsumed by the continuity or synchronization of fundamental patterns or relations.

The Poetic Image begins, like *A Hope for Poetry*, as if it were a study in style. Its subject, however, is neither images nor composition nor criticism, though the book is filled with numerous sensitive readings of poems. The "poetic image" is for Day Lewis a theory of the poem as autonomous, whole, complete—or a microcosm of wholeness in a world of time. He needed the autonomous poem as urgently as did Eliot and the orthodox New Critics, and for an astonishingly similar reason. The fundamental assumption of the English poetic tradition, he argued, is that underlying and relating all things and events there is an order and purposiveness—no less true of an age preoccupied with the science of relativity than of one constituted by a faith in some great chain of being. (He does not go quite so far as Eliot in insisting that this order is substantial and is thus manifest in the Christian view of history as Incarnation; his is rather a kind of vital energy, the electrical attraction of one thing for another, one person for another—in a word, *love*.) *The Poetic Image*, like *A Hope for Poetry*, is another argument for the need of community as the ground of all human value and, hence, as the impulse of poetry.

What Day Lewis tries to account for, then, is the unity within the historical changes of the poetic tradition. Poetry has progressed from primitive song to self-conscious complexity; human consciousness has progressed from superstition (unity) to intellectualism (dualism). But the *need* of community (it is a synonym for *order*) has not altered with the processes of history working against it. Only the forms (including the poetic forms) in which that need is satisfied have changed to accommodate the changes in reality; and yet those forms manifest the one recurring impulse toward wholeness. Even for the modern mind, the invariable of relativism has replaced the old absolutes; and, while modern science goes blithely on its way presuming the immutability of relativity, the modern imagination seeks new poetic forms by way of verifying not modern chaos but the ultimate order within or behind things-as-seen. When Day Lewis argues that the old myths have been replaced by the "myth of the individual" and that the "poetic image" is that myth, he acknowledges the revolutionary poetics of Romanticism (the movement of the center of reality from social objectivity to individual subjectivity); but, more important, he is pointing the way to a post-Romantic poetics in which the need for community (the most universal of human universals) is verified not by logos or telos but by man's ceaseless quests for wholeness and thus a way out of self. He assumes a universal subjectivity—the a priori evident in man's communal as opposed to his private will for order. Everyone is an ancient mariner; his individual quest is for the social, not the private, good. The "poetic image," manifesting wholeness, serves not only its maker but his audience as a symbol of human potentiality.

Poetry, Day Lewis argues in a crucial passage in *Poetic Image*, "always returns to [a collective] consciousness for its sanction. It is not merely that, time and again, we find in the images of modern poetry forms and impulses derived from the myths; but the very nature of the image . . . invokes that consciousness, as though man, even at his most individual, still seeks emotional reassurance from the sense of community, not community with his fellow-beings alone, but with whatever is living in the universe, and with the dead" (32–33). The "collective consciousness" avoids the extreme claims of Jung's archetypal unconscious, but it is no less a mystique of tradition: it is the energy that manifests itself in myths and continues to drive modern man to order his life by fundamental and recurrent patterns. In the book's last chapter, Day Lewis alludes to the "collective consciousness" as an "eternal spirit" that lives only in the wholeness of poems which, whatever their particular experiences, repeated the primordial event of community.

The "collective emotion" or "communal experience" evoked in the reader of poetry, he claims, is the transformation of deeply rooted, unconscious experience into esthetic (hence controlled) emotion—the "recognition" that brings order rather than provoking action (144). "This response," he continues, "registers a satisfaction of the human desire for wholeness. The individual is brought, however remotely, into touch with communal experience, general truths which have eternally bound mankind together" (144). Withdrawal into the world of art is, hence, not solipsistic but a prelude to a new communal rebirth. Thus Day Lewis' theory of the poem as "image": "a poem makes us happy because, being itself a complete thing and so presenting us with a 'hollow image of fulfilled desire,' it creates in us the illusion of completeness. Through our experience of the poem, we are reborn—not indeed complete, for the perfection is the prerogative of art alone in this world—but, because poetry's illusion is a fertile one, a degree or two nearer the wholeness for which our selfhood strives" (145). Man, as Hegel argued is Desire—Desire for the Other—and thus incomplete. Hence, man is action, or time—a seeker of the other. If man cannot be cured of desire, Day Lewis argues here, the poem may be an "illusion" of his cure, and thus the ideal of community forever denied the self. The poem is cleansed of history, but its role is the same: to manifest the "illusion" of wholeness, to point forward yet inward to that ultimate image, the magnetic mountain which is the perfection of art and the image of man's hope.

In short, *The Poetic Image* is another poetics of hope, based upon the purity and wholeness of the poem where alone history is contained and transcended. The illusion that history is purified leaves the reader with the sense it may someday be so, as it ideally once was. *The Poetic Image* accommodates, on the one hand, Day Lewis' materialism and, on the other, his recurring belief in the "eternal spirit," or poetic imagination which saves the self from the knowledge of necessity. The "poetic image" is his Word, his "Word Over All," to recall the phrase he borrowed from Whitman. In speaking to man's common needs, the "image" holds him in the "illusion" of the ultimate community of love to which he aspires. But there is one difference in this "hope for poetry": it is a world *to be composed* by man's "eternal spirit," not one suspended to ideological promise; it is future, to be, and it leaves the poet anxiously in the present with his work to do.

IV   *The Reclaimed Muse*

The consistent argument running through Day Lewis' criticism is that the poet needs a "system" within which to write—one which manifests itself as a received tradition and renders unto the poet a language and social order. "System," in other words, is a sense of history as teleological. But for the modern poet, system is precisely what is missing, and hence his predominant concern is with his need or lack—with his "self" as Desire. Eliot had looked backward nostalgically; and Day Lewis in the 1930's, finding nostalgia irresponsible, could only embrace a futurist myth. But his immediate concern was with the systemless present: for Marxism, while it commanded action in the present, had its magic appeal in the apocalypse of a future. When that magic failed, poets were less disturbed on the whole than were intellectual idealists; for poets could never really afford to ignore the present, and thus could never ignore the inevitable distance between reality and idea. It is not Marx so much as Hegel from whom Day Lewis' poetics derive—the poetics of desire.

In *Transitional Poem*, Day Lewis had dramatized his situation as a conflict between a Spinozistic view of self and a Hobbesian view of self, with the Spinozistic order of mind primary. Ultimately, Day Lewis' materialism wiped out his reliance on the transformative and synthesizing power of "brain" and, with it, one of the fundamental principles of poetic tradition. His recourse to Marxism, while made in the face of brute and dehumanizing historical fact, must certainly be interpreted as a quest for a new system—one in which, this time, materialism is contained in a transcendent and purposive order. In other words, his theme was freedom increasingly cluttered by necessity. Thus the poet, celebrating particular events, could celebrate them not simply in terms of revelation and apocalypse but as present manifestations of a meaningful dialectic—a desire motivating a quest for the other which would take one beyond desire. For a brief time in the 1930's, Marxism promised the journey beyond the self as desire for the entire culture.

Within this frame of reference, it is easier to understand Day Lewis' subsequent shifts of faith—to the mystique of the "poetic image" and finally to the "lyric impulse." For ultimately, the only system available to the poet in the whirl of contemporary process was the poetic imagination—the "tetragonal/ Pure symmetry of brain" of *Transitional Poem* turned inward to the depths of the "collective consciousness." The imagination as "eternal spirit" or "lyric impulse" transcends the personal by linking the social self to a universal human community. That imagination, which lies in the "primary, instinctual self" (152), is the ultimate system; for it, the creator of all systems, is generated out of man's "perpetual need for wholeness" (153), or his "need" to transcend need, desire.

In the opening section of the previous chapter, I discussed the general argument of *The Lyric Impulse*. Though lacking in philosophical depth, the work is unquestionably a valuable summary of the historical life of the lyric genre, but what it tells us about Day Lewis' own development is something else again. His view of the lyric as the "instinctive spontaneity of song" (4) or as a "gift from the goddess" (131); its qualities as "brevity, simplicity, purity" (5), or "a kind of grace" (131); its source in a preurban way of life and in the communal instinct; its impersonality and innocence—these are the qualities of an epiphanic art, the kind Day Lewis may have longed to write, or thought he wrote in his purest moments, but in fact did not. More significantly,

they are qualities of a poetry which exists at the level of pure
community, untouched and uncorrupted by history—a poetry confirming the ultimately abstract system, "wholeness," in which the self is
subsumed by its relationships and quieted of desire. Thus there is no
longer a self or person but only a voice of community, or love.

The "tetragonal/ Pure symmetry of brain" becomes the "lyric
impulse," embodied in the image of the "Muse" or "goddess" who
controls the "golden bridle" of Pegasus:

> The Muse, through she visit her poet but fitfully, is the ground of his
> being. She will not come meekly to his call; but when she does come,
> she possesses him entire, and her absence leaves a void which cannot be
> filled with other preoccupations. He may have no religious belief, may
> even feel no need for god, yet he is religious in the sense that he cannot
> live by material values: though he may not know it, he is the man in
> Browning's poem—the one "Through a whole campaign of the world's
> life and death,/ Doing the King's work all the dim day long."

> To him that work is one of interpretation and creation, and the two
> are inseparable. He has to make out of words an object which is
> distanced from his own personal experience, yet by indirections will
> make sense of it and communicate the feeling of it. (150—51)

The Muse as mother-spirit is the redeemer of materialism, and the
antithesis of history—doing the "King's work." She is the system of
systems, since she is the axial law of all archetypes, the source and
center of the human. Or, to put it another way, she is a metaphor for
the poet's own creative identity in which, through the poetic self, he
transcends his social self. The Muse is the dead God of Christianity, the
lost Logos, or Word, rediscovered.

But Day Lewis' Muse is only a metaphor. He cannot embrace her
intimately, as Graves does his Goddess. And this incapability has made
Day Lewis' poetic career a dedicated venture of escape from self and
thus from the responsibility of his personal creative powers. He has
tried to become impersonal by being a poet so deeply personal that his
private identity would be subsumed by his communal role. His
materialism, his Marxism, his search for "ancestors," his desire for the
impersonal, and his inveterate imitation of other poets—they all resolve
into a strangely coherent poetics of a poet who fears to fall below his
powers. Day Lewis could not fully accept what Erich Heller has called
the "hazard of modern poetry," the responsibility of the poet who
must create value where his universe offers none, who must generate
order where all is incoherence. Day Lewis, that is to say, did not

adequately comprehend the role he assumed: of what it means to "create," especially in a thoroughly materialistic world. At the crucial moments when he was faced with that responsibility, he chose to turn away from a direct confrontation. He has not been, like his modern "ancestors," a revolutionary, and hence has not been a responsible caretaker of tradition. He has not extended the style he inherited, nor made a lasting impression in it. In this sense, he is properly the Poet Laureate, the voice of a community rather than a self.

It is the self-reflexive quality of his poetry, its recurrent self-examination of the problematic of language and thus of the myth of history, that characterizes his modernism. But he was never very comfortable with the role of modern poet, nor self-deceptive enough to think he could escape it. The self-consciousness of his poetry repeatedly indicates that he knew he had to ask more of poetry than it could deliver. In a universe otherwise without a fixed or vital center (without God), the human self must serve as the generating source of order; and the poet assumes his paradigmatic role as the caretaker of that creative energy. And yet the self as center portends an anarchy of selves, an atomistic world, and a terrifying isolation for the creative mind. It implies that the creative imagination is nothing but desire, insatiable desire. Day Lewis' traditionalism, as much as Eliot's traditionalism, testifies to that fear of the ultimate existential freedom and anarchy. Unlike Eliot, however, Day Lewis' world could afford no either/or commitment: neither self nor selflessness; for both, as he recognized of Eliot, denied the human and repudiated history. What Day Lewis demanded was some impossible reconciliation of the two. His poetry stands as evidence of the act of reconciliation—an act in which the problematic of creation, language, and order are the issue.

Day Lewis' poetry turns upon the theme of love, or the search for love. Love is sexual, social; it is communal; it is, above all, the ideal of order, a redeemed history. It is Unity. It is what the poem aspires toward; the wholeness of which the poem is the "illusion." Day Lewis' poems, then, may stand as evidence of the act toward reconciliation; but we certainly do not expect that they achieve reconciliation. For all his distrust of history (that is, his yearning for ideal pasts or consummate futures), his is ultimately the voice of a man who accepts change and hence has the precarious role of trying to define an ever changing self. If the weakness of Day Lewis' poetry is its nostalgia (an obsession with an earlier, buried self—that self which was whole, presumably), its strength is in its humility (its awareness that it is condemned finally to a present of change and a future of death). Out of this sense emerges occasionally a poem poignantly aware of itself—a knowledge constituted in the face of necessity, which, as he predicted early on in *Transitional Poem*, makes him an "orchard god" who is "Grounded in temperate soil" (24).

NOTES AND REFERENCES

Chapter One

1. See Stephen Spender, *World Within World* (London, 1951), pp. 138–39.
2. "Preface," *New Signatures*, collected by Michael Roberts (London, 1932), pp. 7–20.
3. *Ibid.*, pp. 14–15.
4. *Ibid.*, pp. 12–13.
5. *Ibid.*, pp. 18–19.
6. "Poetry in Revolution," *New Country, Prose and Poetry by the Authors of New Signatures*, ed. by Michael Roberts (London, 1933), p. 69.
7. *The Creative Element, A Study of Vision, Despair and Orthodoxy among some Modern Writers* (New York, 1954), p. 13.
8. *World Within World*, pp. 2–3.
9. "Preface," *New Country*, p. 9.
10. "The Education of a Communist," *Left Review*, I (Dec., 1934), 63–64, 66.
11. See "Concerning Marxism" and "Marxism and Philosophy," *Sense and Non-Sense*, trans. Hubert Dreyfus and Patricia Dreyfus (Evanston, 1964), pp. 99–124 and 125–36.
12. Introduction to Julius Lipton, *Poems of Strife* (London, 1936), p. 8.

Chapter Two

1. *Oxford Poetry, 1927*
2. *The Poetics of Space*, trans. by Maria Jolas (New York, 1964), p. 61.
3. "Preface," *Oxford Poetry, 1927*, p. vi.
4. This phrase should be compared with a very similar one from a very different kind of poet, William Carlos Williams: "we can measure between objects," he wrote in a letter to John Thirlwall, "therefore, we know that they exist" (see *The Selected Letters of William Carlos*

Williams, ed. J. Thirlwell [New York, 1957], p. 331). Day Lewis' lines express the fallen, dualistic world, in which the self knows the other as alien, and is involved in a dangerous dialectic with it; while Williams' phrase suggests that reality is a field of "force," in which the self exists objectively, as one of the relational entities which compose that field, for a field is by definition a system of relatives without a definable center.

5. Day Lewis' notes are included in the original version of *Transitional Poem,* published by the Hogarth Press in 1929. This note appears on page 70 of that edition.

6. Pages 70–71, Hogarth Press edition of the poem.

7. In *The Poet's Way to Knowledge* (Cambridge, 1957), pp. 7–8, Day Lewis quotes approvingly Yeats's line about man's love of the transient—"Man is in love and loves what vanishes"—and backs up Yeats with Whitehead's observation about the human urge to be released "into change." He assumes the paradox of man's search for permanence within change to be the animating force of poetry. Thus, his and Auden's repeated use of Engels' paradox that freedom lies in the knowledge or recognition of necessity.

Chapter Three

1. *The Wild Goose Chase* (London, 1944), p. 28. Page numbers included in the text refer to this edition.

2. *World Within World* (London, 1951), p. 191.

3. See *Illusion and Reality* (London, 1946). The book was first published in 1937.

4. "Introduction," *New Signatures,* coll. by Michael Roberts (London, 1932), p. 19.

Chapter Four

1. *Illusion and Reality* (London, 1946), p. 235.

2. *Studies in a Dying Culture* (London, 1938), p. 71.

3. *Ibid.*, p. 46.

4. The original version is not included in the *Collected Poems 1954.* References here are to *A Time to Dance, Noah and the Waters, and Other Poems* (New York, 1936).

5. Foreword, *Noah and the Waters, ibid.*

6. "Revolutionaries and Poetry," *Left Review,* I (July, 1935), 397–402. The essay was later incorporated along with two others into "Revolution in Writing" and printed in *A Time to Dance, Noah and the Waters, and Other Poems, ibid.*

Chapter Five

1. *The Poetic Image* (London, 1947).

2. For the most thorough and penetrating study of the artist's problem in transforming a violent and dehumanizing reality into literary form, see the second major section, "Violence," of Frederick J. Hoffman, *The Mortal No, Death and the Modern Imagination* (Princeton, N.J., 1964).

3. "The Creative Imagination in the World Today," *Folios of New Writing* (London, 1940), p. 157.

4. *The New Republic* (June 24, 1967), 21–24.

5. Clifford Dyment, *C. Day Lewis* (London, 1955), p. 38.

6. Introduction, *Modern Love*, ed. C. Day Lewis (London, 1948), p. xxi.

7. The poem entitled "Emily Brontë" appears in *Poems 1943–1947* (see *Collected Poems*, 278), while the essay called "Emily Brontë and Freedom" may be found in *Notable Images of Virtue* (Toronto, 1954).

8. *Contemporary English Poetry* (London, 1959), p. 92.

9. Introduction, *Modern Love*, p. viii.

10. See "Poetry as Reportage," *Times Literary Supplement* (Mar. 6, 1953), 152.

Chapter Six

1. The apparent new orthodoxy of leftist poets in the 1930's soon produced its countermovement in England, in Lawrence Durrell, Dylan Thomas, and even by the end of the decade, Spender. Kenneth Rexroth's anthology, *The New British Poets* (New Directions, n.d.), is the best evidence of that Romantic revival, which was to manifest itself in America in the 1950's and 1960's as a strong countercurrent to New Criticism and to the academic poetry which had followed in the wake of the "intellectual" poetry of Eliot and the orthodoxy of modernism it had seemed to establish.

2. "It Takes a Hero to Make a Poem," *Interviews with Robert Frost*, ed. by E. C. Lathem (New York, 1966), pp. 172–76.

Chapter Seven

1. In a postscript added to the third edition of *A Hope for Poetry* (Oxford, 1936), Day Lewis devoted himself almost exclusively to the phenomena of "pure" and Surrealistic poetry. Not only was this poetry anticommunal, he argued, and hence irresponsible in a time of crisis, but its renewed vogue in the 1930's seemed to accentuate for Day Lewis the increasing twentieth-century schisms of life and art which his generation of poets had found intolerable and against which it had directed its main energies.

2. *Studies in European Realism*, trans. by Edith Bone (New York,

1964). The introductory essay of this important study is reprinted in *The Modern Tradition*, ed. by Richard Ellmann and Charles Feidelson, Jr. (New York, 1965), 349–60.

 3. Leon Trotsky, *Literature and Revolution* (New York, 1957), p. 170.

 4. *Ibid.*, p. 167. Trotsky sees artistic style as a response to social need and, like Day Lewis, anticipates the changes of poetic style which must accompany historical change. Note that Trotsky asserts the a priori of historical change to stylistic change, thus asserting the preeminent creative force of history rather than the creative self: "Language, changed and complicated by urban conditions, gives the poet a new verbal material, and suggests or facilitates new word combinations for the poetic formulation of new thoughts or of new feelings, which strive to break through the dark shell of the subconscious. If there were no changes in psychology produced by changes in the social environment, there would be no movement in art; people would continue from generation to generation to be content with the poetry of the Bible, or of the old Greeks."

 5. "Mr. Day Lewis' Pale Fire," *The New Republic* (June 24, 1967), 21–24.

SELECTED BIBLIOGRAPHY

(For a complete bibliography see *C. Day-Lewis, the Poet Laureate: A Bibliography*. Compiled by G. Handley-Taylor and Timothy d'Arch Smith. With a letter of introduction by W. H. Auden. Chicago: St. James Press, 1968.)

Primary Sources

I. Books of Poems

Beechen Vigil. London: Fortune Press, 1925.
Country Comets. London: Hopkinson, 1928.
Transitional Poem. London: Hogarth, 1929.
From Feathers to Iron. London: Hogarth, 1931.
The Magnetic Mountain. London: Hogarth, 1933.
A Time to Dance and Other Poems. London: Hogarth, 1935.
Collected Poems 1929–1933. London: Hogarth, 1935.
Noah and the Waters. London: Hogarth, 1936.
Overtures to Death. London: Jonathan Cape, 1938.
Poems in Wartime. London: Jonathan Cape, 1940.
Selected Poems. London: New Hogarth Library, 1940.
Word Over All. London: Jonathan Cape, 1943.
Short Is the Time, Poems 1936–1943. New York: Oxford University Press, 1945.
Poems 1943–1948. London: Jonathan Cape, 1948.
Collected Poems 1929–1936. London: Hogarth, 1948.
Selected Poems. London: Penguin Poets Series, 1951.
An Italian Visit. London: Jonathan Cape, 1953.
Christmas Eve. London: Faber and Faber, 1954. (Ariel Poems).
Collected Poems 1954. London: Jonathan Cape and Hogarth, 1954.
Pegasus and Other Poems. London: Jonathan Cape, 1957.
The Gate and Other Poems. London: Jonathan Cape, 1962.
The Room and Other Poems. London: Jonathan Cape, 1965.
Selected Poems. New York: Harper and Row, 1967.

II. Novels

The Friendly Tree. London: Jonathan Cape, 1936.
Starting Point. London: Jonathan Cape, 1937.
Child of Misfortune. London: Jonathan Cape, 1939.
(Day Lewis has written, under the pseudonym of Nicholas Blake, a number of detective stories. The following list, though perhaps not inclusive, represents the larger part of them: *A Question of Proof* (1935); *Thou Shell of Death* (1936); *There's Trouble Brewing* (1937); *The Beast Must Die* (1938); *The Smiler with the Knife* (1939); *Malice in Wonderland* (1940); *The Case of the Abominable Snowman* (1941); *Minute for Murder* (1947); *Head of a Traveller* (1949); *The Dreadful Hollow* (1953); *The Whisper in the Gloom* (1954); *A Tangeled Web* (1956); *End of Chapter* (1957); *A Penknife in My Heart* (1958); *The Widow's Cruise* (1959); *The Worm of Death* (1961); *The Morning After Death* (1966).

III. Books of Criticism

A Hope for Poetry. Oxford: Basil Blackwell, 1934.
The Poetic Image. London: Jonathan Cape, 1947. (The Clark Lectures for 1946).
Notable Images of Virtue: Emily Brontë, George Meredith, W. B. Yeats. Toronto: Ryerson Press, 1954. (Chancellor Dunning Trust Lectures, Queens University, Ontario, 1954).
The Lyric Impulse. Cambridge, Mass.: Harvard University Press, 1965; London: Chatto and Windus, 1965. (The Charles Eliot Norton Lectures for 1964—65).

IV. Miscellaneous: Translations, Published Lectures, Pamphlets, Editions, Anthologies, Contributions to Periodicals, and Introductions

Oxford Poetry, 1927. Ed. with introd. by W. H. Auden and C. Day Lewis. New York: Appleton and Co., 1928.
Dick Willoughby. Oxford: Basil Blackwell, 1933. (A story)
"Controversy," *Left Review*, I (Jan, 1935), 128—29.
"Revolutionaries and Poetry," *Left Review*, I (July, 1935), 397—402.
"Revolution in Writing," London: Leonard and Virginia Woolf, Hogarth, 1935. (Day to Day Pamphlet, No. 29). Also see *A Time to Dance, Noah and the Waters, and Other Poems*. New York: Random House, 1936. Pp. 61—96. (This American collection of his poems, which was published in two editions in England, included this three-part essay, the third of which was "Revolutionaries and Poetry." The first, "The Revolution in Literature," was initially presented as a broadcast talk in the Youth Looks Ahead Series; the second was entitled "Writers and Morals.")

"English Writers and a People's Front," *Left Review*, II (Oct. 1936), 671–74.

"We're *Not* Going to Do Nothing: A Reply to Mr. Aldous Huxley's Pamphlet 'What Are You Going to Do About it?' " *Left Review Pamphlet*, 1936.

"Labour and Fascism: The Writer's Task," *Left Review*, II (Nov., 1936), 731–33.

"Sword and Pen," *Left Review*, II (Dec., 1936), 794–96.

Introduction to Julius Lipton, *Poems of Strife*. London: Lawrence and Wishart, 1936. Pp. 7–12.

Imagination and Thinking. Life and Leisure Pamphlets: No. 4. London: British Institute of Education, 1936. (With L. Susan Stebbing).

Selected Poems by Robert Frost. Introductory essays by W. H. Auden, C. Day Lewis, Paul Engle, and Edwin Muir. London: Jonathan Cape, 1936.

"An Expensive Education," *Left Review*, III (Feb., 1937), 43–45.

"Gerard Manley Hopkins, Poet and Jesuit," *Left Review*, III (April, 1937), 172–75.

"Tinker," *New Writing*, III. London: Lawrence and Wishart, 1937. (A short story)

"Goings-on in Gloucestershire," *Left Review*, III (June, 1937), 273–75.

The Echoing Green, an anthology of verse for children between the ages of eleven and fourteen. 3 Vols. Oxford: Basil Blackwell, 1937.

Ralph Fox, A Writer in Arms. Ed. John Lehmann, T. H. Jackson, and C. Day Lewis, with an introduction by C. Day Lewis. London: Lawrence and Wishart, 1937.

The Mind in Chains, Socialism and Cultural Revolution. Ed. with introduction by C. Day Lewis. London: F. Muller, 1937.

Anatomy of Oxford. London: Jonathan Cape, 1938. (With Charles Fenby).

The Georgics of Virgil. Trans. by C. Day Lewis. London: Jonathan Cape, 1940.

A New Anthology of Modern Verse, 1920–1940. Ed. with introduction by C. Day Lewis and L. A. G. Strong. London: Methuen, 1941.

Poetry for You, A Book for Boys and Girls on the Enjoyment of Poetry. Oxford: Basil Blackwell, 1944.

The Colloquial Element in English Poetry. The Literary and Philosophical Society of Newcastle-upon-Tyne, 1947.

Enjoying Poetry. London: Cambridge University Press, 1947.

Introduction to Lilian Bowes Lyon, *Collected Poems*. London: Jonathan Cape, 1948.

Introduction to George Meredith, *Modern Love*. London: Rupert Hart-Davis, 1948.

The Otterbury Incident. London: Putnam, 1948. (Adaptation of the French film *Nous les gosses*, a children's detective story)

"The Lyrical Poetry of Thomas Hardy," *Proceedings of the British Academy, 1951,* XXXVII. London: Geoffrey Cumerledge, 1951. Pp. 155–74. (Wharton Lecture on English Poetry)

The Poet's Task. Oxford: Clarendon Press, 1951. (His first lecture as holder of the Oxford Chair of Poetry)

The Grand Manner. Nottingham: University of Nottingham Press, 1952. (Byron Foundation Lecture)

The Aeneid of Virgil. Trans. by C. Day Lewis. London: Hogarth, 1952.

The Chatto Book of Modern Poetry, 1915–1955. Ed. by C. Day Lewis and John Lehmann. London: Chatto and Windus, 1956.

"The Poetry of Edward Thomas," *Essays by Diverse Hands,* XXVIII. Ed. by Angela Thirkell. London: Geoffrey Cumberledge, 1956. (The Giff Edmonds Memorial Lecture)

The Poet's Way of Knowledge. Cambridge: Cambridge University Press, 1957. (The Henry Sidgewick Memorial Lecture for 1956)

The Buried Day. London: Chatto and Windus, 1960. (Autobiography)

A Book of English Lyrics. Ed. by C. Day Lewis. London: Chatto and Windus, 1961.

The Collected Poems of Wilfred Owen. Ed. with introduction and notes by C. Day Lewis. London: Chatto and Windus, 1963.

The Eclogues of Virgil. Trans. by C. Day Lewis. London: Jonathan Cape, 1963.

A Need for Poetry. University of Hull, 1968. (Lecture)

On Translating Poetry. Abbey Press, 1970.

SECONDARY SOURCES

CAUDWELL, CHRISTOPHER. *Further Studies in A Dying Culture.* Ed. with a preface by Edgell Rickword. London: Bodley Head, 1949. Posthumously published essays by one of England's youngest and most promising Marxist critics, Christopher St. John Sprigg, who was killed in Spain.

————. *Illusion and Reality, a Study of the Sources of Poetry.* Lawrence and Wishart, 1946. Caudwell's most famous book, first published in 1937 shortly after his death; an ingenious exploration of the historical evolution of literature in terms of its role in the human and social economy. Literature, for Caudwell, is both a response to a need and a manifestation of the struggle to satisfy that need; thus it is instrumental to the spiritual as well as to the actual economy of any culture.

————.*Studies in a Dying Culture.* Introd. by John Strachey. London: Bodley Head, 1938. Essays supplementing *Illusion and Reality,* five of them on individual moderns who manifest for Caudwell the symptoms of contemporary decadence, the bourgeois illusion, and the like.

DAICHES, DAVID. *Poetry and the Modern World*. Chicago: University of Chicago Press, 1940. Daiches devotes an entire chapter to Day Lewis and divides a chapter between Auden and Spender, indicative of the respect he holds for Day Lewis' clear and direct moral stand in the 1930's and particularly for a poetry of action. Equally indicative is Daiches' distrust of Yeats for his refusal to confront directly the age.

DEUTSCH, BABETTE. *This Modern Poetry*. New York: W. W. Norton, 1935. A few brief remarks, particularly of the Hopkins and Owen influence on Day Lewis, of the poetic movement of the early 1930's.

DURRELL, LAWRENCE. *A Key to Modern British Poetry*. London: Peter Neville, 1952. More valuable for an understanding of Durrell than for its views of modern British poetry; offers but passing commentary on Day Lewis.

DYMENT, CLIFFORD. *C. Day Lewis*. London: Longmans, Green, and Co., 1955. This pamphlet, in the British Council's Writers and Their Work Series, is the closest thing to a full-scale work on Day Lewis. It is, however, only a moderately long essay, an appreciative survey of Day Lewis' work up through *An Italian Visit*.

FROST, ROBERT. "It Takes a Hero to Make a Poem," *Interviews with Robert Frost*. Ed. by E. C. Lathem. New York: Holt, Rinehart, and Winston, 1966. Revealing dialogue about Day Lewis' own search for the heroic in the modern world.

GLICKSBERG, CHARLES I. "Poetry and Marxism: Three English Poets Take Their Stand," *University of Toronto Quarterly*, VI (April, 1937), 309–25. In general, an assessment of how Day Lewis, Auden, and Spender looked left without embracing any prescribed dogma.

HENDERSON, PHILIP. *The Poet and Society*. London: Secker and Warburg, 1939. A negative view; very much obsessed with the alleged irresponsibility of the Auden Group's preoccupation with games and Kiplinesque heroics.

LEHMANN, JOHN. *The Whispering Gallery, Autobiography I*. New York: Harcourt, Brace, 1955. Especially valuable for its reminiscences, and for its recounting of Lehmann's association with the Hogarth Press, his founding of *New Writing*, and his relations with other writers, like Day Lewis.

LIFSHITZ, MIKHAIL. *The Philosophy of Art of Karl Marx*. Trans. by Ralph B. Winn. New York: Critics Group, 1938. An interesting document, recounting not only Marx's esthetics but the manner in which those esthetics were read in the 1930's in relation to the social philosophy. Sees the history of art as a progressive decline, from the world of Homerean unity to the present.

MANDER, JOHN. *The Writer and Commitment*. London: Secker and

Warburg, 1961. Lengthy chapter on Auden offers some limited perspectives on Day Lewis' commitment in the 1930's.

MACNEICE, LOUIS. *Modern Poetry, A Personal Essay.* London: Oxford University Press, 1938. Attacks art-for-art's sake "escapism" and identifies the Georgian emphasis on simplicity, health, nature and the like, with the esthetes' emphasis on ravage, decadence, and suicide. Good view of what poets in the 1930's were reacting against.

New Country, Prose and Poetry by the Authors of NEW SIGNA-TURES. Ed. by Michael Roberts. London: Hogarth Press, 1933. A sequel to *New Signatures*; more aggressively leftist and activist. Contains four poems from Day Lewis' *The Magnetic Mountain* and a prose piece, "Letter to a Young Revolutionary."

New Signatures, Poems by Several Hands. Collected with introduction by Michael Roberts. London: Hogarth, 1932. The first gathering of the Auden Group. Included three poems by Auden, three by Julian Bell, seven by C. Day Lewis, five by Richard Eberhart, six by William Empson, four by John Lehmann, seven by Spender, two by William Plomer, and six by A. S. J. Tessimond.

New Writing. Ed. by John Lehmann. London: The Bodley Head, 1936–38. First published in 1936, the First Series included five volumes, a volume published twice yearly through the spring of 1938. Proclaimed itself anti-Fascist but of no political party. Its primary interest was literature. Volume III carried an announcement that no criticism would be published. In 1938, a Second Series began, published by the Hogarth Press, that ran through three volumes. Thereafter, appeared at irregular intervals as *Folios of New Writing*.

PRESS, JOHN. *The Chequer'd Shade, Reflections on Obscurity in Poetry.* London: Oxford University Press, 1958. Passing comments on poets of the Auden Group, stressing particularly their dislike for the contemporary world yet their devotion to tradition.

REPLOGLE, JUSTIN. "The Auden Group," *Wisconsin Studies in Contemporary Literature*, V (Summer, 1964), 133–50. More valuable for historiography than for criticisms; nonetheless, an informative and useful presentation of the basic facts related to this group that was not a group.

————. "The Auden Group: The 1930's Poetry of W. H. Auden, C. Day Lewis, and Stephen Spender. Unpublished Ph.D. dissertation, University of Wisconsin, 1956. Important collection of details about the Auden Group and a general critical overview of themes, images, and preoccupations of the three poets.

————. "The Gang Myth in Auden's Early Poetry," *Journal of English and Germanic Philology*, LXI (July, 1962), 351–61.

Useful also in explaining something of this same "myth" in Day Lewis' poetry.

RICKWORD, EDGELL. "Who Is This Noah?" *Left Review*, II (April, 1936), 339–40. Negative review of *Noah and the Waters* but more significant as an indication of the way the more dogmatically committed Marxists viewed the bourgeois poet's "heresies": "The theory of contemplation as the essence of poetic vision is the reflection of the squeezing out of the poet from social-political life which has been going on now for a century."

ROBERTS, MICHAEL. *Critique of Poetry*. London: Johathan Cape, 1934. Extended version of the views Roberts set forth in his introduction to *New Signatures* (1932).

ROSENTHAL, M. L. *The Modern Poets, A Critical Introduction*. New York: Oxford University Press, 1960. Largely introductory; concentrated on the 1930's.

ROSS, ROBERT S. *The Georgian Revolt, Rise and Fall of a Political Ideal, 1910–1922*. Carbondale: Southern Illinois University Press, 1965. Useful historical survey of the English literary world during Day Lewis' formative years.

SCARFE, FRANCIS. *Auden and After, The Liberation of Poetry 1930–1941*. London: Routledge, 1942. One of the first books to treat the Auden Group and its impact. No longer an important document, it devoted its first chapter to "The Development of Day Lewis."

SPENDER, STEPHEN. *The Creative Element, A Study of Vision, Despair, and Orthodoxy among some Modern Writers*. New York: British Book Center, 1954. Good index of the movement of activist writers in the 1930's beyond a social poetry. Written as a corrective to his 1930's book, *The Destructive Element*, denying especially that an engagement of political crisis necessarily implies a corrective. Rejects the partisanship of a literature of action.

————. "The Creative Imagination in the World Today," *Folios of New Writing*. London: Hogarth, 1940. Argues that the poet needs an orthodox system in which to contain modern chaos but indicates that political orthodoxy, lacking the element of mystery that sustains religious orthodoxy, offers too strict a mold for the imagination and hence harms creation.

————. *The Destructive Element, A Study of Modern Writers and Belief*. London: Jonathan Cape, 1936. One of the most important, and most revealing, pieces of criticism written in the 1930's. Concerned primarily with Eliot's criticism of the modern artist's loss of belief and tradition, but it denies him the privilege of mythicizing the past. Contains a brilliant, but wrong-headed, attack on Henry James.

————. *Forward from Liberalism*. New York: Random House, 1937. A haltingly developed total philosophy of the postliberal intellectual, or the intellectual who must be not only the reservoir of tradition but the active agent of his culture's rebirth. An activist's prolegomenon.

————. Introduction. *Poems for Spain*. Ed. S. Spender and John Lehmann. London: Hogarth, 1939. Pp. 7—14.

————. *World Within World*. London: Hamish Hamilton, 1951. Perhaps the most valuable of the memoirs of the 1930's; important not only for its information about the writer and the time but also for Spender's particular interpretation of the events—and for what he does not say.

STRACHEY, JOHN. "The Education of a Communist," *Left Review*, I (Dec., 1934), 63—69. Highly revealing statement by one of the foremost English Communists about the roots of his ideology, emphasizing the moral dislocations of the world he grew up in as opposed to either social or economic causes of his political beliefs.

STRONG, L. A. G. "Cecil Day Lewis," *Personal Remarks*. London: Peter Neville, 1953. An appreciation mainly; applauds Day Lewis' lyrical talents and his personal as opposed to political poetry.

SWINGLER, RANDALL. "History and the Poet," *New Writing*. N.S. III. London: Hogarth, 1939. Assessment of the poet's task in the decade that had passed.

SYMONS, JULIAN. *The Thirties, A Dream Revolved*. London: Cresset, 1960. Reminiscences, by a prominent author-critic, of what it meant to be a writer in that decade.

THWAITE, ANTHONY. *Essays on Contemporary English Poetry*. London: Heineman, 1959. Rather superficial overview of the subject; passing remarks on the Auden Group.

TSCHUMI, RAYMOND. *Thought in Twentieth-Century English Poetry*. London: Routledge and Kegan Paul, 1951. Tschumi offers a rather lengthy chapter on Day Lewis' philosophical development, especially in the 1930's, but he sticks mainly to exposition and does not probe deeply the implications of the "philosophy." Tschumi does recognize the continuity between Day Lewis' social conscience and his idealism, pointing out the way in which emotion supplants intellect as the poet develops. Substantial readings of the major poems.

WOOLF, VIRGINIA. *A Letter to a Young Poet*. London: Hogarth Press, 1932. Famous advice to young poets (mainly Spender, but also Auden and Day Lewis), admonishing them for publishing too soon and for sacrificing a concern with the purity of their craft in their haste to make literature purify the world.

Index

Arnold, Matthew, 79
"Auden Group," vii, 17-22, 26, 30, 61, 76, 131, 137
Auden, W. H.: "Ballad of Miss Edith Gee, The," 91; *Poems,* 19; "Which Side Am I Supposed to Be On?" 60; mentioned, vii, 17, 18, 19, 23, 25-26, 27, 28-29, 30, 32, 35, 36, 39, 40, 41, 42, 47, 50, 56, 58, 59, 62, 63, 68, 75, 79, 80, 85, 86, 91, 107, 111, 113, 132, 135, 136, 138

Bachelard, Gaston, 46
Bell, Clive, 19
Bell, Julian, 19, 78
Bell, Vanessa, 19
Bible, The, 51
Blake, Nicholas (pseudonym for C. Day Lewis), viii
Blake, William, 70
Brontë, Emily, 104
Brooke, Rupert, 43

Caudwell, Christopher (Christopher St. John Sprigg): *Illusion and Reality,* 148n; *Studies in a Dying Culture,* 148n; mentioned, 32, 70-71, 75-76, 77, 78, 79, 117, 137, 138
Communist Manifesto, 30, 84
Contemporary English Poetry, 149n
Cornford, John, 75
Cummings, E. E., 132
Day Lewis, Cecil: Poet Laureate, vii, viii, x, 17; the problem of language, viii, 20, 37-38, 48, 55-57, 106-7, 137ff.; the "lyric impulse," viii, 116-21, 141ff.; search for a

metaphysical "system," 20, 26-27, 36, 37, 96, 123, 138-39, 142-43; the divided self, 22, 38, 52, 60, 76, 101-15 *passim*; transition and the journey, 22, 38, 39, 41, 46-47, 59-62, 63ff., 69ff., 96, 101-3, 134ff., 139; between Lawrence and Marx, 28-36, and *passim*; the meanings of death, 36, 65, 67, 81-83, 90ff., and *passim*; desire, 52ff., 75, 82, 142, and *passim*; as "war poet," 96ff.

WRITINGS OF:

"Almost Human," 123
"Ariadne on Naxos," 122
"Assertion, The," 100-01
"Baucis and Philemon," 122
Beechen Vigil, 26, 43-44, 116
"Behold the Swan," 88
"Bombers," 77, 88, 90
Buried Day, The, 18, 19, 22, 23, 25, 27, 30, 32, 43, 46, 64, 75, 76, 87, 124
"Carol, A," 81
"Christmas Eve," 125
"Circus Lion," 128
Collected Poems, 1954, 80-81, 85, 99, 115, 148n
"Committee, The," 123
"Conflict, The," 76, 79-80
Country Comets, 26, 39, 43-45
"Cyprian! Cyprian," 45
"Dedham Vale, Easter, 1954," 125
"Departure in the Dark," 101
"Double Vision, The," 104, 106
"Ecstatic, The," 80

"Emily Brontë," 104, 149n
"Ending," 106
"Failure, A," 106
"Father to Sons," 125
From Feathers to Iron, 19, 30, 31, 33, 36, 37, 58, 59, 63-68, 69, 111
Gate, The, 118, 126-29
"Gate, The," 127
"Heart and Mind," 106
Hope for Poetry, A, 28, 35, 43, 70, 76, 86, 95, 117, 118, 133, 134-39, 140, 149n
"House Where I Was Born, The," 123-25
"In Me Two Worlds," 76, 79
Italian Visit, An, ix, 109-15, 118
"Johnny Head-in-Air," 76, 80
"Juvenilia," 106
"Late Summer," 44
"Learning to Talk," 80
"Light House, The," 101
"Losers," 80
"Lost," 44
Lyric Impulse, The, 86, 116-20, 121, 126, 133, 143-45
Magnetic Mountain, The, 31, 32, 36, 37, 58, 59, 68-74, 75
"Marriage for Two," 106, 107
"Married Dialogue," 106, 107
"Moods of Love," 125-26
"Moving In," 78-79
"My Love Came to Me," 45
"Nabara, The," 77, 90-91, 93
"Naked Women of Kotyle," 45
"Net, The," 43-44
"Newsreel," 77, 88, 89-90
"New Year's Eve," 107-8
"Night Piece," 88
Noah and the Waters, 83-87
Notable Images of Virtue, 149n
"O Dreams, O Destinations," 101-3
"Once in Arcady," 44
"Only Pretty Ring-Time, The," 45
"On Not Saying Everything," 121, 126-27
Overtures to Death, 36, 88-94, 95, 99
"Overtures to Death," 77, 88, 91-94
"Passage from Childhood," 88-89
Pegasus and Other Poems, 118, 120-26

"Pegasus," 122-23
"Pietà," 129
Poems in Wartime, 99
Poems 1943-1947, 103-9
Poetic Image, The, 35, 95-96, 97, 98, 100, 109, 114, 116, 118, 119, 120, 133, 139-42, 149n
Poet's Way of Knowledge, The, 120-21, 148n
Preface, to *Oxford Poetry, 1927,* 18, 27, 41-42, 48, 56, 105, 135
"Retrospect: From a Street in Chelsea," 45
Room, The, 118, 121, 122, 126, 129-30
"Room, The," 129
"Rose-Pruner," 44
"Saint Anthony's Shirt," 129-30
"Sanctuary," 44
"Sheepdog Trials in Hyde Park," 128
"Sketches for a Self-Portrait," 106-7
"Son and Father," 125
"Spring Song," 88
"Stand-To, The," 100
Starting-Point, 25
"Three Cloud-Maidens, The," 88
Time to Dance, A, 76, 78-83, 111, 148n
"Time to Dance, A," 77, 80-83
Transitional Poem, 19, 25, 27, 28, 29, 37, 39, 40, 41, 42, 43, 46-57, 58-59, 60, 63, 68, 76, 84, 98, 108-9, 143, 146, 148n
"View from an Open Window," 127-28
"Warning to Those Who Live on Mountains, A," 80
"Watching Post," 100
"Woman Alone, The," 106, 107
Word Over All, 99-103, 139
"Word Over All," 100, 142
"Wrong Road, The," 123

Donne, John, 50, 53, 63
Durrell, Lawrence, 149n
Dyment, Clifford, 99, 149n

Eliot, T. S.: *Murder in the Cathedral,* 85; "Tradition and the Individual Talent," 21; *Waste Land, The,* 67;

mentioned, 18, 21, 25, 26, 34, 40, 42, 47, 48, 51, 62, 63, 64, 74, 97, 98, 114, 134, 138, 139, 140, 145, 149n

Emerson, Ralph Waldo: "Each and All," 45

Empson, William, 19

Engles, Frederick, 78, 82

Fenby, Charles, 23, 25

Folios of New Writing, 149n

Forster, E. M., 79, 88

Freud, Sigmund, 27, 28, 111

Frost, Robert: "Road Not Taken, The," 123; mentioned, 113, 123, 128-29

General Strike, the, 25

Graves, Robert, 118, 144

Groddeck, Georg, 27, 29, 111

Hardy, Thomas, 44, 104, 108, 113, 123, 139

Hedges, L. P., 81-82

Hegel, G. W. F., 32, 33, 35, 142

Heller, Erich, 144

Hoffman, Frederick J.: *Mortal No, The,* 149n

Hopkins, Gerard Manley, 40, 45, 70, 71, 134, 139

Interviews with Robert Frost, 149n

Isherwood, Christopher, 85

Jung, Carl, 140, 141

Keats, John, 112, 115, 125

King, Mary, 50

Lane, Homer, 27

Lawrence, D. H.: *Psychoanalysis and the Unconscious,* 63; mentioned, 28-36, 51, 66, 70, 76, 78, 94, 117, 137

Leavis, F. R., 118

Left Review, 24, 77, 82, 86, 147n

Lehmann, John, 19

Lévi-Strauss, Claude, 115

Lewis, Wyndham, 137

Lipton, Julius: *Poems of Strife,* 147n

Lukacs, Georg: *Studies in European Realism,* 135; 149n

MacNeice, Louis, 132

"Macspaunday," 131, 132

Maritain, Jacques, 41

Marlowe, Christopher, 81

Marshall, Margaret, 50

Marx, Karl, 28-36, 70, 87, 111, 135, 137

Marxism, 21, 24, 25, 26, 28-36 *passim,* 75, 76, 78, 84ff., 87-88, 92, 98, 108, 135ff.

Maximian, 47

Melville, Herman, 47

Meredith, George: *Modern Love,* 104, 105, 106, 149n; mentioned, 104, 105, 106, 108, 123, 139

Merleau-Ponty, Maurice: *Sense and Non-Sense,* 32; 147n

Milton, John, 51

More, Jasper: *Land of Italy, The,* 109

Muir, Edwin, 87

New Country, 77, 147n

New Republic, The, 149n, 150n

New Signatures, 147n, 148n

Noah (in Day Lewis' poems), 52, 84ff.

Owen, Wilfred, 40, 45, 134, 139

Oxford Poetry, 1927, 18, 27, 39, 41-42, 48, 56, 105, 135, 147n

Poe, E. A., 101

Pope, Alexander, 78

Richards, I. A., 42, 56, 118

Roberts, Michael, 19-20, 24, 74, 147n, 148n

Shakespeare, William, 51

Shelley, Percy Bysshe, 112, 115

Spender, Stephen: *Creative Element, The,* 147n; *Destructive Element, The,* 76; *World Within World,* 18, 24, 147n, 148n; mentioned, 17, 18, 19, 20, 22, 24, 68-69, 75, 77, 98-99, 132, 149n

Spinoza, Benedict, 48, 50
Steer, G. L.: *The Tree of Gernika,* 90
Strachey, John, 24-25

Tessimond, A. J. S., 19
Thomas, Dylan, 113, 123, 132, 149n
Thwaite, Anthony, 104
Times Literary Supplement, 149n
Trotsky, Leon: *Literature and Revolution,* 137; 150n

Upward, Edward: *Journey to the Border,* 61

Valéry, Paul: "La Cimetiere de marin,"

108; mentioned, 38, 40, 108, 121, 126, 128
Virgil: *Georgics,* 71

Wadham College, Oxford University, 23, 26
Wain, John, 99, 139
Warner, Rex: *Wild Goose Chase, The,* 61-62, 148n; mentioned, 19, 23, 25, 40, 50, 61-62, 70
Whitehead, A. N., 41, 43, 48
Whitman, Walt, 47, 50
Williams, William Carlos, 121, 147n
Woolf, Virginia, 19, 68
Wordsworth, William, 44, 63

Yeats, W. B.: "Second Coming, The," vii; mentioned, 34, 47, 50, 63, 113